A Remedial English Grammar for Foreign Students

by

Frederick T. Wood

MACMILLAN
PUBLISHERS

First published 1965
Reprinted 1967, 1968 (twice), 1970,
1971 (twice), 1972, 1973, 1974 (three times), 1978 (twice),
1979, 1981, 1984, 1986

Published by *Macmillan Publishers Ltd*
London and Basingstoke
Associated companies and representatives in Accra, Auckland, Delhi, Dublin, Gaborone, Hamburg, Harare, Hong Kong, Kuala Lumpur, Lagos, Manzini, Melbourne, Mexico City, Nairobi, New York, Singapore, Tokyo

ISBN 0-333-09425-5

Printed in Hong Kong

PREFACE

This book does not set out to be a complete grammar of the English language. Its aim, as the title implies, is to concentrate on, and to attempt to correct, the most frequent grammatical mistakes made by foreign students of English. To some extent, of course, the difficulties experienced, and the mistakes most frequently made, vary according to the nationality and the mother tongue of the students concerned, but there are quite a large number which are common to almost all, and it is with these that the present book deals. They have been suggested by those experienced in the teaching of English as a foreign language, and by foreign students themselves with whom the writer has been in touch either personally or by correspondence. Thanks are also due to Mr Ronald Ridout, who read the entire typescript and made a number of useful suggestions.

A feature of the book is the provision of ample exercises to give the student practice on each point as it arises. The explanatory matter has been made as concise and simple as possible, and illustrative examples have been given of each point dealt with.

The tendency of modern linguistic teaching is to avoid as far as possible the type of exercise which involves substitution or the mere filling in of blank spaces within the framework of a given sentence; and in general the present writer is in full sympathy with this tendency. The inclusion in the present book of so many exercises of this kind can, however, be justified by the purpose they are intended to serve and the aim of the book as a whole—the correction of specific mistakes and the removal of particular difficulties. If the student is given a free hand he is likely to avoid the difficulties; if he is to master them by constant practice he must be kept to the point all the time. It is to help him in this way that the exercises have been devised. If he wishes, of course, the teacher can supplement them by others of his own to meet the needs of a particular group.

Sheffield F. T. W.

PREFACE

[illegible]

CONTENTS

1. The articles

A. THE DEFINITE ARTICLE (*THE*)

1 Do not put *the* before the names of substances if they are used in a general sense.

> Gold is a precious metal. (not *the gold*)
> Bread is made from flour. (not *the bread....the flour*)
> Lead is very heavy. (not *the lead*)

But *the* must be used if the reference is to a particular kind or specimen of the substance.

> The gold mined here is of poor quality.
> They were grateful for the bread we gave them.
> Thieves stole the lead from the roof.

(Similarly: sand, butter, cheese, milk, grass, meat, paper, rice)

The nature of the particular kind or specimen need not always be stated; it may sometimes be understood from the situation, or from what has been said previously.

> If you will pay for the bread, I will pay for the meat.
> (i.e., the bread and the meat that we need, or that we have recently had)

2 Do not put *the* before the names of meals if they refer to the meals generally, as a part of the daily routine.

> Breakfast is at eight o'clock. (not *the breakfast*)
> When do you have dinner? (not *the dinner*)
> Have you had lunch yet? (not *the lunch*)

But *the* must be used:

(*a*) When the meal is a particular one, thought of as a social function.

> The dinner will be held at the Grand Hotel.

(*b*) When the name of the meal refers to the food rather than the occasion.

We enjoyed the breakfast she gave us.
The dinner was not properly cooked.

N.B. The name of a meal may be preceded by a possessive adjective (my, your, his, her, their, its) if we wish to give it a personal application.

I was having my lunch when they arrived.
She always has her breakfast in bed.
It's time I gave this dog its dinner.

3 Do not put *the* before plural nouns when they are used in a general or a universal sense.

Apples are grown in many different countries. (not *the apples*)
Books are essential to a student. (not *the books*)
Aeroplanes can fly very fast. (not *the aeroplanes*)

But if the reference is to particular ones, then *the* must be used.

The apples on our tree are not yet ripe.
The books you gave me will be most useful.

The is also used when the reference is to all of the things mentioned, but only within a particular country or area. The country or area need not be stated; it may be implied in the context.

The recent frosts have damaged the cherries.

4 Do not put *the* before the names of games.

I play football. (not *the football*)
Chess is a game which requires great skill and patience. (not *the chess*)

(Similarly: cricket, rugby, tennis, hockey, polo, baseball, cards, whist, draughts, dominoes, ludo)

5 Do not use *the* before the names of countries unless the name suggests that the country is made up of smaller units or constituent parts.

France, Italy, China and Ghana are all republics. (not *the France, the Italy, the China, the Ghana*)

But: The United States is one of the great world powers.
(Similarly the following must have the article:
the United Kingdom, the Soviet Union, the U.S.S.R., the U.S.A., the Netherlands.)

We also say *the* Sudan and *the* Transvaal, although the names do not suggest that they are composed of smaller units.
An article is also necessary if the name of the country is preceded by the word *Kingdom, Republic, Protectorate, Federation.*

The Kingdom of Macedon, The Republic of South Africa.

6 Do not use *the* before the words *King* and *Queen* if they are followed by the name of the king or queen.

King George V, Queen Victoria, Queen Elizabeth II (not *the King George V, the Queen Victoria, the Queen Elizabeth II*)

The same applies to *Pope.*

Pope John (not *the Pope John*)

King George V and Queen Elizabeth II are read as *King George the Fifth* and *Queen Elizabeth the Second.*
Similarly: Richard III (Richard the Third), Henry IV (Henry the Fourth), Edward VII (Edward the Seventh)

7 *The* may be used before a name which ends in *Road* where the name is also a place-name, but it may also be omitted.

I bought this watch at a shop in the Edgware Road.
or I bought this watch at a shop in Edgware Road.

But it must not be used before names ending in *Street, Avenue, Crescent* or *Lane:* nor is it used before the name of a square, or a road where the name is not a place-name.

There are many large shops in Oxford Street. (not *the Oxford Street*)
Nelson's monument is in Trafalgar Square. (not *the Trafalgar Square*)

To avoid confusion, the student is advised to omit *the* before *Road* also. But it must not be omitted when *road*—in this case spelt with a small letter—is not part of the name, but means ' the road that leads to. . . . whatever place is named '.

> When you get to the outskirts of Dover, take the London road.

8 Put *the* before nouns which name the inhabitants of a country collectively or as a community, but not before the names of their languages.

> The French live in France, and the Portuguese in Portugal. (not *French live in France, and Portuguese in Portugal.*)
> The Russians sent up the first earth satellite. (not *Russians sent up* . . . .)

(Similarly: the British, the English, the Chinese, the Germans, the Dutch, the Italians, the Indians)

> The inhabitants of France speak French. (not *the French*)
> Spanish is spoken in Spain. (not *the Spanish*)

(Similarly: English, German, Russian, Italian, Chinese, Hindustani, Urdu, Serbo-Croat, Polish)

Plural nouns standing for the people of a particular country, however, are not preceded by *the* if the people in question are thought of individually.

> Indians have dark skins.
> Russians drink vodka.

In some cases one noun is used for the collective sense, and a different one for the individual sense.

> *the English*, but *Englishmen; the French*, but *Frenchmen*; *the British*, but *Britons; the Spanish*, but *Spaniards; the Irish*, but *Irishmen*.

9 Put *the* before the names of mountain ranges, or ranges of hills, but not before the names of single mountains or hills. (For exceptions to this rule, see below.)

> The Alps, the Himalayas, the Pyrenees, the Pennines, the Cotswolds

But: Everest, Mont Blanc, Snowdon (not *the Everest, the Snowdon*)

As exceptions to this rule we always say: *the Matterhorn, the Jungfrau.*

10 Use *the* before the names of rivers, canals, seas, oceans, valleys, deserts and forests.

London is on the Thames. (not *on Thames*)
Many ships use the Kiel Canal. (not *use Kiel Canal*)

(Similarly: the North Sea, the Pacific, the Baltic, the Ganges, the Rhine, the Sahara, the Ardennes, the Black Forest)

But when the name of a river forms part of the name of a town that stands on it, *the* is not used.

Stratford-upon-Avon, Newcastle-upon-Tyne, Kingston-on-Thames, Burton-on-Trent

11 Use *the* before the names of municipal or government departments and before the names of shops, business houses, industrial concerns, banks etc., except when they begin with a personal name.

The Westminster Bank, the Ministry of Education, the public library, the Grand Hotel, the War Office, the Army and Navy Stores

But:

Barclays Bank, Lloyd's Bank, Selfridge's, Woolworth's, Clark's Picture Gallery

We always say *the* Albert Hall, however, in spite of the fact that it begins with a personal name; and the same applies to a few other well-known halls, e.g. the Usher Hall.

The names of railway stations, when they are also place names, as most of them are, are not preceded by *the*.

Euston Station, St. Pancras Station, Lime Street Station (Liverpool), New Street Station (Birmingham)

We speak of Waterloo Station and Victoria Station (in London) because the names have been given to the surrounding districts, though they took their names from the battle of Waterloo and from Queen Victoria respectively. There are Victoria Stations in several other large towns, and these are usually referred to locally as ' *the* Victoria Station '.

Note: Cambridge University, Sheffield University, etc., but the University of Cambridge, the University of Sheffield.

12 Though, following the rule given above, the name of a large store or works may not take the definite article, its sub-departments do.

> The travel department at Harrod's
> The overseas department of Lloyd's Bank
> The melting shop at Hadfield's Foundry

13 Use *the* before the names of ships and trains, even if they do not form part of the name itself.

> The *Queen Elizabeth* is a famous British liner.
> The *Golden Arrow* is an express train which runs from London to Paris each day.

But when the name of a particular type of vehicle is used to name a means of travel, there is no definite article.

> We are going to London by train.
> I go to work by bus.
> The fastest means of travel is by aeroplane (or *by air*).

14 *The* is left out of the expressions *all day* and *all night*, but it should be used in similar adverbial expressions for other divisions of time: *all the morning*, *all the afternoon*, *all the evening*, *all the week*.

> I have worked hard all day. (not *all the day*)
> The nurse stayed up all night with the patient. (not *all the night*)

But:

> It has been raining all the morning.

Americans often say *all morning*, *all week*, etc. This is now frequently heard in England also, and is becoming normal British usage.

15 *The* is used before a singular noun to express what we call ' the generic singular ', i.e., the one thing mentioned is taken to represent all of that kind.

> The tiger and the cat belong to the same family of animals.
> The elephant is very strong.
> The aeroplane is the fastest means of travel that is in common use.

N.B. An exception to the above rule is the noun *man* when it is used to denote the human race as a whole.

> Man is the only creature that has developed the power of speech. (not *the man*)
> Man does not live by bread alone.

16 Note the omission of *the* in such expressions as *go to school, go to church, go to hospital, go to prison.* There are parallel expressions which use *the*, but in the case of these latter the reference is merely to the building. When *the* is omitted, the reference is to the purpose for which the building exists.

> The children go to school.
> If you are seriously ill you will have to go to hospital.

But:

> The stranger went to the school to complain about the behaviour of one of the pupils.
> I am going to the hospital to visit a sick friend.

We always say *go to work*, but *go to the office.* (not *go to office*)

EXERCISES

1 Fill in the blank spaces in the following sentences with the word given in brackets at the end, using either the plain noun, or the noun preceded by *the* (whichever you think is correct).

a The box was made of .... (wood)
b Some coins are made of .... and some of .... (silver, copper)
c .... in that stream is not suitable for drinking. (water)
d .... is found in Australia and South Africa. (gold)
e .... that we had for dinner was tough. (meat)

f In Britain more people drink .... than .... (tea, coffee)
g When do you have ....? (breakfast)
h There is fish for .... today. (dinner)
i Are you attending .... tonight? (dinner)
j .... are grown in Spain. (oranges)
k We wear .... to keep us warm. (clothes)
l .... are not allowed to park here. (cars)
m .... in that vase are very beautiful. (flowers)
n Let us have a game of .... (cricket)
o She plays .... very well. (tennis)
p What are we having for ....? (lunch)
q .... in that field is very green. (grass)
r Do you usually drink .... or ....? (tea, coffee)
s .... are used in some countries to pull heavy loads. (elephants)
t She thanked me for .... I gave her. (present)

2 Fill in the blank spaces in the following sentences with the word or words given in brackets at the end. Use either the plain noun, or the noun preceded by *the* (whichever you think correct).

a In Austria the people speak .... (German)
b .... is spoken in many countries. (English)
c .... have been a sea-faring people for many centuries. (English)
d Can you speak .....? (French)
e .... are a very musical nation. (Italians)
f Many great ships cross .... (Atlantic Ocean)
g .... is a very large country in .... (India, Asia)
h We arranged to meet outside .... (Woolworth's)
i His uncle is manager of .... in this town. (Overseas Bank)
j He came for an hour, but stayed all .... (evening)

3 Take each of the following nouns and compose two sentences in which it is included. In the first sentence use the plain noun (i.e., without *the*), in the second the noun preceded by *the.*

air, iron, rice, flour, meat, water, paper, grapes, horses, boys

4 In the following passage a number is placed in each of the blank spaces. Fill in the space with the word or expression which has the same number in the list given at the foot of the passage. Insert *the* before the word or expression if you think it necessary.

My uncle lives in a large house built of (1). He works in (2) of (3), which is situated in (4). He goes there by (5) every morning, and stays there all (6). When he comes home in (7) he often feels tired. As soon as he gets in he has a cup of (8), and after that he feels refreshed. When he has had a meal he sits down and reads (9) which he bought on his way home. When he has finished with (10) he will sit listening to (11), or smoking. He sometimes smokes a pipe, but he prefers (12).

List of words and phrases to be inserted

1. stone	5. bus	9. newspaper
2. local office	6. day	10. newspaper
3. Barclays Bank	7. evening	11. radio
4. East Street	8. coffee	12. cigarettes

5 Fill in the blank spaces in the following sentences with the noun given in brackets at the end. Insert *the* before the noun wherever you think it necessary.

a He was found guilty of theft and sent to . . . . for six months. (prison)
b My son will be old enough to go to . . . . next May. (school)
c I must go to . . . . to see the headmaster. (school)
d My wife has gone to . . . . to visit a sick friend. (hospital)
e He is very ill, and has to go to . . . . (hospital)
f John is ill, so he cannot go to ..... (school)
g I feel tired, as I went to ..... late last night. (bed)
h In Britain many people do not go to ..... on Saturday morning. (business)
i I no longer go to ..... on Saturdays. (office)
j I have not been to ..... for several months. (cinema)
k Some of the visitors came by ....., others by ..... (train, bus)
l Are you going to India by ..... or by .....? (sea, air)
m We sail tomorrow on ..... (*Dunbar Castle*)

B. THE INDEFINITE ARTICLE (*A* and *AN*)

1 Remember that *a* is used before words beginning with a consonant, and *an* before words beginning with a vowel or with a letter *h* which is not sounded. The following is a list of the chief words in English which are spelt with an unsounded *h*.

> Heir, heiress, heirloom, honest, honesty, honorarium, honorary, honour, honourable, honoured, hour, hourly.

The *h* of hotel is now generally sounded. Write *a hotel*. *An hotel* is rather old-fashioned.

2 *A*, not *an*, must be used before words which begin with a vowel symbol pronounced with the same sound as the *y* in *yet*.

Such words are: Europe, European, uniform, union, unique, Unitarian, united, universal, university, usual.

> Switzerland is a European country. (not *an European*)
> I hope to go to a university. (not *an university*)

3 Do not omit *a*/*an* before a singular noun standing for things that can be counted.

> Rice is *a* cereal. London is *a* city. *A* dog is *an* animal.

A/*an* must also be used when the noun is preceded by an adjective. In such cases it goes before the adjective.

> London is a big city. (not *London is big city*)
> A lion is a dangerous animal. (not ..... *is dangerous animal*)

Not only are living creatures, plants, material objects, and natural features such as rivers, lakes, hills and seas countable; so also are such things as rewards, punishments, penalties and salaries. They must therefore have the article before them when used in the singular.

> He was given a reward for his bravery.
> If you are promoted, you will get a higher salary.
> The court imposed a heavy penalty.

A is not normally used before nouns standing for things that cannot be counted, but it may be used before such nouns if the reference is to:
(*a*) a particular kind of the thing;

I like a white wine with my lunch.

or (*b*) a particular quantity.

Let's go into this restaurant and have a coffee. (i.e., a cup of coffee.)

4 The names of professions and occupations take the indefinite article.

My brother is a teacher. (not ..... *is teacher*)
I hope to be a doctor. (not *I hope to be doctor*)

The same rule applies to nouns such as *hero*, *genius*, *fool*, *thief* and *liar*, which describe someone by telling us the kind of person he is.

Beware of that fellow; he is a thief. (not .... *he is thief*)

5 The indefinite article always follows the word *such* when it is applied to things that are countable.

I have never known such a wet summer. (not *a such wet summer*)
Such a thing has never happened before. (not *a such thing*)

6 If an adjective is preceded by *so*, the *a* or *an* must be placed between the adjective and the noun.

I have never known so wet a summer. (not *a so wet summer*)

7 When *a* is placed before the word *few* it changes the meaning. *Few* means only a small number, when more might have been expected; *a few* means a small number when none might have been expected.

Few pupils gave the right answer. (i.e., I had hoped for more)

A few pupils gave the right answer. (i.e., They did not all, as one might have supposed, give the wrong answer.)

There is a similar difference between *little* and *a little.*

We have little time to spare. (i.e., not so much as we should like)
We have *a* little time to spare. (i.e., We are not so short of time that we have none to spare.)

Adverbs such as *only* and *just* can be used before *a few* and *a little*, but not before *few* and *little.*

There are just a few apples left.
We have only a little money.

EXERCISES

1 Insert *a* or *an* in the blank spaces in the following sentences.

a ..... elephant is a very strong animal.
b He had always hoped that his son would go to ..... university.
c Italy is ..... European country.
d I shall be back in less than ..... hour.
e Is there ..... hospital in this town?
f Everyone respects ..... honest person.
g By ..... united effort we may achieve success.
h I like to give ..... useful present.
i I understand he is to marry ..... heiress.
j ..... honour was conferred on him for his services to his country.
k We stayed at ..... hotel in the centre of the town.
l It is ..... great honour to be invited to such a gathering.
m The door was opened by ..... servant.
n ..... honorary secretary is one who is not paid for his services.
o He was carrying ..... heavy load.
p There is ..... hourly bus service on this route.
q ..... big dog dashed out of the gate.
r We shall come if we get ..... opportunity.
s That was not ..... very honest thing to do.
t The proposal was accepted by ..... unanimous vote.

2 Complete the following sentences by inserting in the blank spaces the words or phrases given in brackets, either with or without the article *a* (or *an*) (whichever you think correct). If you insert *a* or *an*, make sure you put it in the right place.

a New York is ..... (large city)
b Bernard Shaw was ..... (famous English dramatist)
c Ice is ..... (frozen water)
d We have had ..... (very tiring journey)
e I have never known such ..... (hot weather)
f Have you ever seen so ..... as that? (tall man)
g I have never heard such ..... (absurd story)
h We shall get ..... next year. (longer holiday)
i It gives me .... to do it. (pleasure)
j He took ..... over the work. (great care)
k My younger brother is ..... (student)
l He hopes to become ..... when he has finished his course. (teacher)
m China is ..... country. (very large)
n John's ambition is to be ..... (engineer)
o I had never been in so ..... before. (large house)

3 Insert *little* or *a little*, *few* or *a few* in the following sentences.

a We have only ..... minutes to spare.
b Could you lend me ..... books.
c He has many enemies, but ..... friends.
d Mr Brown was a man of ..... words.
e The ground is very dry, as there has been ..... rain for the past ..... months.
f A busy person has ..... time to spare.
g We will stay here for .... while.
h I have spent nearly all my money, and have only .... left.
i As the matter is outside our control, there is ..... we can do about it.
j You should be able to do the job if you have .... patience.

2. Agreement of verb and subject

A verb must agree with its subject in number and person. In this connexion the following are some important points to remember.

1 In the present tense of most English verbs the third person singular ends in *-s*, but there is no *-s* on the third person plural.

A cow eat*s* grass.	My friend like*s* swimming.
Cows eat grass.	My friends like swimming.

The chief exceptions to this rule are *he is—they are*, where different words are used, and *he does—they do*, *he goes—they go*, where the singular ending is not *-s*, but *-es*, because the previous letter is a vowel. *Can*, *may*, *must* and *ought*, and the auxiliaries *will* and *shall* do not have *-s* on either the singular or the plural.

He will do it if you ask him.
They will do it if you ask them.

But when *will* is a full verb, and not an auxiliary, it follows the rule for most other verbs, and takes the ending *-s* on the third person singular.

Whatever God wills, man cannot alter.

Note that in verbs that end in *y* preceded by a consonant (fly, try, pity), the *y* is changed to an *i* and *-es* is added.

A bird flies.
He tries.
She pities the unfortunate child.

2 When the subject is *one of*, followed by a plural noun (one of the teachers, one of the employees), the verb is singular, to agree with *one*. There is often a temptation to make it agree with the plural noun that immediately precedes it, but this is incorrect.

One of my teachers lives next door to my aunt. (not *live*)
One of my friends has a fine collection of postage stamps. (not *have*)

3 If a clause or any other long group of words separates the subject from the verb, special care is necessary to remember the actual subject-word, and to make the verb agree with it.

> *All the books* which have been placed on that table by the window *need* re-binding.
>
> *The radio* which you gave my children works perfectly.

4 When the subject is the formal *there*, the verb agrees with the ' real ' subject that follows it. (See also p. 108.)

> There *is* no reason to doubt his honesty.
> There *are* thirty pupils in our class.

5 Normally, when a subject consists of two or more nouns, it has the force of a plural, and takes a plural verb.

> John and Mary *have* gone for a holiday.
> Barley, wheat and rice *are* cereals.

But when two or more nouns represent a compound name of one thing, then the compound is thought of as singular, and takes a singular verb.

> Bread and butter *is* a wholesome food.
> There'*s* eggs and bacon for breakfast.

6 Similarly when a plural number applies to distances, weights, heights or amounts of money, and represents a single figure or quantity, it is treated as a singular and takes a singular verb.

> Ten pounds *is* a lot of money. (not *are*)
> Twenty miles *is* not a great distance in these days of rapid travel. (not *are*)
> Two pounds of coffee *costs* seven and sixpence. (not *cost*)

7 If the title of a literary work, or the name of a house or a hotel, is a plural, for purposes of agreement it is treated as a singular, since it is only one title or one building.

> *The Thirty-Nine Steps* was written by John Buchan.
> The Rose and Crown is situated in the High Street.

EXERCISES

1 Insert the correct form of the present tense of the verb in the blank spaces in the following sentences. The verb to be used is given in brackets at the end of each sentence.

a A new car ..... a lot of money. (cost)
b Most things ..... more now than they did a few years ago. (cost)
c Jet aeroplanes ..... very fast. (fly)
d An aeroplane ..... more quickly than a bird. (fly)
e The countryside ..... very beautiful in spring. (look)
f Those children ..... very healthy. (look)
g One of the players ..... from the same village as myself. (come)
h In Britain many workers ..... to work in their own cars. (go)
i All the pupils in our school ..... English. (learn)
j The owner of that factory ..... very rich, and ..... in a large house. (be, live)
k One of the pupils in our class ..... a motor cycle. (own)
l Some people ..... travelling by sea, as it ..... them sea-sick. (dislike, make)
m The postman ..... each morning with the letters. (call)
n A snail ..... very slowly. (move)
o All the books on that shelf ..... to me. (belong)
p Her aunt and uncle ..... a house in the country. (have)
q Four ounces ..... the smallest quantity we sell. (be)
r Apple pie and custard ..... my favourite dish. (be)
s Ten miles ..... a long way to walk. (be)
t The tallest of the three boys ..... next door to me. (live)

2 Insert *is* or *are* after the word *there* in the following sentences.

a There ..... many rooms in that large hotel.
b There ..... several pages missing from this book.
c If you want some sugar, there ..... some in that basin.
d There ..... eleven players in a football team.
e There ..... nothing to be afraid of.
f There ..... a cause for everything.
g There ..... no lamps in this street.
h There ..... several bookshops in our town.

i There ..... little hope of his coming now.
j There ..... a fierce dog in that yard.

3 Insert *was* or *were* after *there* in the following sentences.

a There ..... a thunderstorm last night.
b There ..... much damage done to the crops.
c There ..... several people in the room.
d There ..... an accident here last week.
e There ..... many fine paintings at the exhibition.

3. Nouns: singular or plural? Some special cases

1 Collective nouns such as *a group* (of things), *a crowd* (of people), *a herd* (of cattle), *a flock* (of sheep), *a regiment* (of soldiers), *a congregation* (of worshippers) are usually singular, even when followed by the *of* adjunct, and they therefore generally take a singular verb.

> A group of people *was* standing at the street corner.
> A flock of sheep *was* grazing in the field.

But sometimes, if we think of the members of the group individually, a plural verb may be used.

> A flock of sheep *were* straying all over the road and causing confusion amongst the traffic.
> The audience *are* requested to leave by the nearest exit.

In the first of these two sentences the plural is used because some of the sheep were straying in one direction and some in another, so that we think of individual sheep, not of the flock as a whole. In the second, though the request is made to the audience as a body, they will not leave as a single body. Some will go out by one exit and some by another.

2 ' Class ' nouns such as *clothing*, *food*, *furniture*, *crockery*, *cutlery*, *stationary* and *footwear* are singular, and must therefore take a singular verb.

> The furniture *is* to be delivered today.
> Sheffield cutlery *has* long been famous the world over.

3 *A pair of*, when applied to things where the two components are always thought of together (scissors, shears, shoes, gloves, trousers) is singular.

> That pair of scissors *belongs* to me. (not *belong to me*)
> A pair of shoes *was* standing in the corner.

But if we omit the words *a pair of* and merely use the plural word, then, of course, it must take a plural verb.

> Those scissors *belong* to me.
> His trousers *were* torn.
> His shoes *were* dirty.

4 *A lot of*, *a great deal of*, *plenty of*, *most of* and *some of* are singular when they refer to amount or quantity, but plural when they refer to number.

> A lot of people prefer tea to coffee.
> A lot of work has still to be done.
> There are plenty of opportunities for well qualified people.
> There is plenty of room on the back row.

5 *People* and *cattle* are plural.

> People do not like to be kept waiting.
> The cattle were grazing in the meadow.

6 *News*, though it has a plural form, is always treated as a singular, and *advice* is never used in the plural.

> What is the latest news?
> No news is good news.
> He gave me much good advice. (not *many good advices*)

7 Names of certain ailments and of certain sciences or branches of knowledge which end in *-s* are also singular: *measles, mumps, shingles, mathematics, physics, economics, ethics.*

Mumps is a serious illness for grown-up people. (not *are*)
Physics is an important subject in the modern world.

N.B. When *mathematics* means ' mathematical calculations ' and *economics* means ' economic facts ', the words are plural.

The area of the room is 160 square feet, if my mathematics are correct.
The economics of the situation have been discussed at some length.

EXERCISES

1 Supply the correct form of the verb (present tense) in the following sentences. The infinitive of the verb to be used is given in brackets at the end of each sentence.

a All the food ..... been eaten. (have)
b A large crowd ..... expected at the football match. (be)
c These shoes ..... almost worn out. (be)
d A pair of gloves ..... been found in the hall. (have)
e Good cutlery ..... expensive. (be)
f A great number of people ..... visited the exhibition. (have)
g A lot of money ..... to be spent on repairs to the house. (need)
h Most of the houses in this street ..... been built within the last twenty years. (have)
i Most of the money ..... now been spent. (have)
j Ill news .... fast. (travel)
k These scissors ..... sharpening. (need)
l All the luggage ..... now been inspected by the customs officials. (have)
m A lot of these apples ..... bad. (be)
n A lot of time ..... been wasted. (have)
o Good advice ..... not always heeded. (be)

2 Supply an appropriate verb to fill the blank spaces in the following sentences.

a The people waiting for the train ..... getting impatient.
b Mathematics .... his weakest subject.

c There ..... plenty of time before the bus leaves.
d There ..... plenty of books on that subject.
e Most of the candidates ..... passed their examination.
f The food we took with us ..... insufficient.
g His trousers ..... covered with mud.
h The whole herd of cattle ..... to be sold.
i A pair of trousers ..... hanging over the chair.
j Warm clothing ..... necessary in cold climates.
k All the furniture in the house ..... old-fashioned.
l Most of the land in this part of the country ..... uncultivated.
m A pair of spectacles ..... lying on the table.
•*n* The stationery ..... been ordered, but ..... not yet been delivered.
o An epidemic of measles ..... broken out in the district.

4. The partitive use of *of*

1 *One of*, *two of* (or any other number of), as well as *many of*, *several of*, *the majority of*, must be followed by a plural noun or pronoun.

One of the boys in our class has won a prize.

Notice that the verb in this sentence (*has*) is singular, because the subject is *one*, not *boys*. But if the number is greater than one, then the verb must be plural, to agree with this number.

Two of the boys in our class have won a prize.
Several of the pupils were awarded scholarships.

2 *Some of*, *half of* (and any other fraction of) take a plural verb if the reference is to number (i.e. to things that are countable), but a singular verb if the reference is to amount or quantity (i.e., non-countables).

Some of the houses are not fit to live in.
Some of the water was spilt on the floor.
Half of the apples were bad.
Half of the land was uncultivated.

3 *The majority of* can be used only for number (i.e., for countable things), not for amount or quantity. In the latter case *most of* must be used.

> The majority of boys like playing football.
> Most of the stain came out of the dress.

Most (as the superlative of *many*) can also be used for things that are countable.

> Most of the houses in this street are new.

4 *Many* refers to number, and is plural; much refers to amount or quantity, and is singular.

> Many of the flowers *are* dead.
> Much of the countryside *was* under water.

5 When *of* is followed by a ' class ' noun such as *clothing, furniture, luggage, traffic, crockery,* which is singular, it cannot be preceded by a word denoting number, only by one denoting amount.

> Some of my clothing has been damaged. (not *several*)
> Much of the furniture is old-fashioned. (not *many*)
> Little of the crockery has been broken. (not *few*)
> Most of the traffic goes by the main road. (not *many*)

EXERCISES

Select from the words given in brackets at the end of each of the following sentences the one which you think should be used to fill the blank space.

1. One of his ..... has been injured in a railway accident. (friend, friends)
2. We have now heard ..... of the evidence. (the majority, most)
3. I have decided to sell ..... of my furniture. (some, several)
4. One of the climbers ..... injured in a fall. (were, was)
5. Some of the luggage ..... not yet arrived. (have, has)
6. Several of my friends ..... been to Britain. (have, has)
7. One of the ..... had several pages missing. (book, books)
8. ..... of the money has now been spent. (many, much)
9. Most of the visitors ..... strangers to me. (were, was)

10. Most of the time ..... spent looking round the shops. (was, were)
11. Each of the pupils ..... given two exercise books. (were, was)
12. ..... of the fruit ..... been damaged by the frost. (some, several: have, has)
13. Much of what he says ..... untrue. (are, is)
14. One of the ..... escaped from the circus. (elephants, elephant)
15. One of the ..... injured. (player was, players were, players was)

5. Concord of nouns, pronouns, and possessive adjectives (third person)

1 If the number is singular, persons of the male sex are referred to by *he*, *him*, *his*, *himself*, persons of the female sex by *she*, *her*, *hers*, *herself*. Non-living things, and most animals (though see under **4**, below), are referred to by *it*, *its* and *itself*.

2 If the noun could refer to persons of either sex (*person*, *pupil*, *scholar*, *reader*, *pedestrian*) the pronouns for the masculine are generally used.

A reader likes to choose his books himself.
A motorist should take great care of his car.

But if, in a particular context, it is clear that the reference is to a woman or a girl, then, of course, the feminine form must be used. The word *member* could, for instance, refer to persons of either sex or both, but when it refers to a member of a women's organisation it is obviously feminine.

There is only one member who has not paid her subscription, and she has promised to pay within the next week.

The words *baby* and *child*, which refer to either sex, are hardly thought of as suggesting sex at all, and so are usually referred to by *it*.

The nurse picked up the baby and gave it to the mother.
The small child was crying for its mother.

3 If the number is plural, persons of either sex, as well as non-living things, are referred to by *they, them, their, theirs, themselves.*

4 An animal is usually referred to by the neuter *it*, even if the noun that is used is one that denotes specifically one sex (e.g. cow, bull).

We watched the cow as *it* placidly chewed the grass.
Don't annoy that bull, or *it* may attack you.

But if there is something in the context or situation which draws attention to the sex of the animal, then *he* or *she* may be used.

In the corner of the shed there was a cow with *her* calf.

Pet animals, which are thought of almost as members of the family, are usually referred to by the pronoun appropriate to their sex.

We have lost our dog. Have you seen him/her?

5 Remember that *every*, and words beginning with *every-* (everyone, everybody, everything) are singular, and must therefore be referred to by the singular pronouns.

Every student passed his examination. (not *their*)
Everyone had to show his ticket. (not *their tickets*)

6 Remember that the possessives *his* and *her*, and the other words derived from them, must agree in gender with the words to which they refer back (or, to put it another way, with the genitive noun that they replace). The use of the masculine, feminine or neuter form does not depend on the gender of the noun that follows it, or that it qualifies.

John gave a present to *his* mother. (not *her mother*)
Susan gave a present to *her* mother, as well as to her father. (not *his father*)

The purse was restored to *its* owner. (not *his owner* or *her owner*).

In the first sentence the possessive takes its gender from *John*, therefore it must be *his*. In the second it takes its gender from *Susan*, therefore it must be *her*. In the third it takes its gender from *purse*, therefore it must be *its*.

If you learn the following table it will help you to use the right pronoun or adjective.

man, boy, everyone, everybody, a person	he, him, his, himself
woman, girl, every woman, every girl	she, her, hers, herself
a thing, an animal	it, its, itself
one	one, one's, oneself
men, women, people, animals, things	they, them, their, theirs, themselves

The table above gives only the third person. That below gives you all the various forms that the personal pronouns and the words derived from them can take, for all persons, and for both singular and plural.

Personal Pronoun		Possessive* Adjective	Possessive* Pronoun	Reflexive Pronoun
Nom.	Acc.			
I	me	my	mine	myself
you	you	your	yours	yourself
he	him	his	his	himself
she	her	her	hers	herself
it	it	its	its	itself
one	one	one's	one's	oneself
we	us	our	ours	ourselves
you	you	your	yours	yourselves
they	them	their	theirs	themselves

*The possessive adjective is used before a noun.
my book, your pen, our dog

The possessive pronoun is used when no noun follows.
This book is mine. Is this pen yours? That dog is ours.

EXERCISES

1 Insert the correct pronoun or possessive adjective in the following sentences.

a John has returned the book which you lent .....
b You must write ..... essays more carefully
c The dog followed ..... master wherever ..... went.
d The children have gone for a holiday with ..... parents.
e Mary had misplaced ..... handbag.
f Could you please lend ..... your dictionary?
g He spoke so softly that we could not hear .....
h We offered to help ..... in their difficulty.
i It was very kind of ..... father to give ..... a lift in ..... car.
j Those girls are very fond of ..... dog.

2 Insert *his*, *her*, *its* or *their* in the blank spaces in the following sentences.

a The little boy was crying because he had lost ..... mother.
b Joan is two years older than ..... brother.
c The two children were waiting for ..... father to return.
d Mr Smith has taken ..... wife to the seaside in the hope that it will improve ..... health.
e The manager asked the visitors into ..... office.
f The faithful dog kept guard over ..... injured master.
g Mary and ..... two brothers have gone to visit ..... aunt.
h Peter spent all ..... week's pocket money on a birthday present for ..... sister.
i The headmistress interviewed the pupils one by one in ..... study.
j He is very proud of ..... daughter's success in ..... examination.
k Two women had ..... handbags stolen during the showing of the film.
l She told me that ..... necklace was a present from ..... husband.
m No-one likes ..... word to be doubted.
n The stray kitten was found by a policeman and restored to ..... mistress.
o All the guests signed ..... names in the visitors' book which the manager kept in ..... office.

3 After each of the following sentences you will find printed a possessive adjective and a possessive pronoun. Insert whichever of them you think correct in the blank space (or spaces) in that sentence.

a Have you seen ..... pen anywhere? (*my, mine*)
b I saw a pen lying in the table, but I don't think it was ..... (*your, yours*)
c ..... car is bigger than ..... (*your, yours: our, ours*)
d That hat is Susan's, but this one is ..... (*my, mine*)
e We sat under the shade of a tree and ate ..... sandwiches. (*our, ours*)
f They should not have spent that money, as it was not ..... (*their, theirs*)
g Those children are very fond of ..... dog. (*their, theirs*)
h While I was on ..... holiday I met a friend of ..... (*my, mine, your, yours*)
i We should always be careful in the choice of ..... friends. (*our, ours*)
j Mary declared that the book was not ..... She would have recognised it if it had been, for she had written ..... name on the fly-leaf. (*her, hers*)

6. The possessive adjective or the definite article with nouns denoting parts of the body

1 When the reference is a general one, and no specific person is indicated, then *the* must be used.

> Drugs have a tendency to dull the brain and affect the heart.
> Scientists tell us that the eye has developed from a sensitive nerve spot.

2 When the reference is to a particular person, or particular persons, the possessive adjective is usually necessary.[1]

She has cut her finger. (not *the finger*)
Hold out your hand. (not *the hand*)
My brother has broken his leg. (not *the leg*)
The children were sent to wash their hands. (not *the hands*)

3 But when the person in question has already been mentioned as the object or the indirect object of a verb, then *the* is used to particularise the part of the body.

His assailant hit him on the head with a stick.
He refused to look me in the face.
I gave him a punch on the nose.

4 With passive verbs the same rule applies when the person in question has been mentioned as the subject.

The victim had been stabbed in the back with a dagger.
The prisoner was chained by the ankle to a log of wood.
He was kicked on the shin while playing football.

5 The names of ailments and diseases of parts of the body always have *the* before the part of the body concerned.

cancer of *the* lung, hardening of *the* arteries, inflammation of *the* throat.

EXERCISES

Fill in the blank spaces in the following sentences with the appropriate possessive adjective or the definite article *the* (whichever you think is correct).

1. If you know the answer, put up ..... hand.
2. When she fell off her bicycle she injured ..... arm.
3. The stone struck him on ..... knee.
4. As he went to kick the ball, he slipped, and twisted ..... ankle.

---

1. But *the* may be used to distinguish a particular one when the limb, or feature mentioned is one of a pair.

He had a scar on the right cheek.
He is slightly lame in the left leg.

5. He gave me a dig in ..... ribs.
6. Sheila is suffering from a cold in ..... head.
7. I have cut ..... finger on a piece of glass.
8. The dog was wagging ..... tail.
9. The policeman grabbed the thief by ..... arm.
10. Reading in a poor light may injure ..... eyes.
11. Excessive smoking is thought to cause cancer of ..... lung.
12. The intruder could not be recognised, as he had a mask over ..... face.
13. You should always give ..... mind to the work you are doing.
14. Reading broadens ..... mind.
15. There are some people who write with ..... left hand.
16. The mother was carrying a baby in ..... arms.
17. He was struck on ..... head by a piece of falling masonry.
18. It has been said that great thoughts arise from ..... heart, but emerge from ..... head.
19. Unless you have something sensible to say, you had better hold ..... tongue.
20. The porter was carrying a heavy burden on ..... back.

7. Confusion of adjectives and adverbs

A. ADJECTIVAL COMPLEMENTS

1 The verbs *to be*, *to seem*, *to become*, and any other verbs with a similar meaning to these three, (appear, feel, look, grow, turn—when it means ' become ') are followed by an adjective, not by an adverb. This is because the word is a complement used to qualify the subject, not to modify the verb.

This year oranges are scarce. (not *scarcely*)
He became very angry. (not *angrily*)
The milk turned sour. (not *sourly*)
The sky grew dark. (not *darkly*)
The problem is really a difficult one, though it appears simple. (not *simply*)

Some of these verbs are also used in a different sense, when they may need an adverb.

> He turned quickly. (not *quick*)
> Those rose trees have grown very rapidly. (not *rapid*)
> The newcomer appeared quite suddenly. (not *sudden*)

Here *turn*, *grow* and *appear* do not mean ' become ' or ' seem ', but ' move round ', ' increase in size ' and ' come into sight ' respectively; hence an adverb, not an adjective, must follow them.

2 An adjective, not an adverb, must also be used after verbs such as *feel*, *sound*, *taste*, *smell* to denote a quality which is experienced or appreciated by one of the physical senses.

> The surface of this table feels rough. (not *roughly*)
> That barrel sounds hollow. (not *hollowly*)
> This fruit tastes bitter. (not *bitterly*)
> That coffee smells good/strong. (not *well/strongly*)

We may say *The bottle smelt strongly of vinegar*, but here the adverb *strongly* means ' to a high degree '.

EXERCISES

1 Fill in the blank spaces in the following sentences with one of the words given in brackets at the end.

a The weather has turned very ..... (warm, warmly)
b At the sound of my voice he turned round ...... (quick, quickly)
c She seems very ..... in her new job. (happy, happily)
d We shall have to make haste, for time is growing .... (short, shortly)
e This kind of tree grows very ..... (slow, slowly)
f Mary's dress looks very ..... (pretty, prettily)
g If you feel ..... come nearer the fire. (cold, coldly)
h His new novel is due to appear ..... (short, shortly)
i The signature on the letter appears quite ..... (genuine, genuinely)
j It feels very ..... in this room. (hot, hotly)
k The speaker congratulated the prize-winners ..... on their success. (warm, warmly)

l Her story sounds ..... (true, truly)
m He turned ..... upon his accusers. (angry, angrily)
n The weather will remain ..... for the next few days. (cold, coldly)
o The crowd became very ..... when the winning goal was scored. (excited, excitedly)
p She looked ..... through all the papers on her desk (careful, carefully)
q This room smells ..... of tobacco smoke. (strong, strongly)
r That soup smells very ..... (appetising, appetisingly)
s Our new neighbours seem very ..... (pleasant, pleasantly)
t He was very ..... to tackle the intruder single-handed. (brave, bravely)

2 For each of the following verbs compose two sentences. In the first sentence the verb is to be followed by an adverb, and in the second by an adjective used as a complement. Any tense of the verbs may be used.

go; come; turn; appear; grow; feel; look; sound

B. WORDS ENDING IN *-LY*

Many adverbs, especially those of manner, are made by adding the suffix *-ly* to an adjective:

foolish, foolishly, quick, quickly, slow, slowly

But if the adjective itself ends in *-ly* it is not usually possible to do this. Such words fall into two classes.

1 Those which are used as both adjectives and adverbs without any change. These include the following words: *daily*, *early*, *fortnightly*, *hourly*, *leisurely*, *nightly*, *only*, *weekly*, *yearly*.

They came by an early train.
They came early. (not *earlily*)

The Times is a daily newspaper.
The Times is published daily. (not *dailily*)

There is an hourly service of buses.
The buses run hourly. (not *hourlily*)

2 Those which can be used as adjectives only. These include: *brotherly*, *cowardly*, *fatherly*, *friendly*, *gentlemanly*, *godly*, *goodly*, *homely*, *likely*, *lonely*, *lovely*, *manly*, *motherly*, *seemly*, *unseemly*, *womanly*. For these the adverbial notion, where one is possible, must be expressed by the phrase *in a ..... ly way* (or *manner*, or *fashion*).

> She was a very friendly person.
> She greeted us in a very friendly manner. (not *very friendly*)
> Such behaviour is unseemly.
> They behaved in an unseemly manner. (not *unseemly*)

The adjective *kind* gives the adverb *kindly*. But there is also an adjective *kindly*, and for this the adverbial equivalent is *in a kindly manner*.

> She was a person of a very kindly disposition.
> She received us in a very kindly manner.

EXERCISES

1 Give the second sentence in each of the following pairs the same meaning as the first by completing it with an adverb or an adverb phrase.

a He is an early riser. He rises .....
b There is an hourly service of trains to the City. The trains to the City run .....
c She gave us a friendly greeting. She greeted us .....
d Your friend is a very gentlemanly person. He always behaves .....
e The doctor paid daily visits to the sick man. The doctor visited the sick man .....
f Mrs Jones was a homely person. She entertained her guests .....
g Most manual workers receive a weekly wage. Most manual workers are paid .....
h The old gentleman gave the child a fatherly smile. The old gentleman smiled at the child .....
i I have taken this house on a monthly rental. I pay the rent .....
j That was a cowardly thing to do. That was behaving .....

2 For each of the following words compose two sentences. In the first sentence the word is to be used as an adjective, and in the second as an adverb.

only; weekly; poorly; early; leisurely

C. *HARD, HARDLY; LATE, LATELY; MOST, MOSTLY*

The adjectives *hard*, *late* and *most* each have two adverbial counterparts, and they must not be confused.

Hard (adverb) means 'diligently, strenuously'. It normally follows the verb.

> You have worked hard today. (not *hardly*)
> He tried hard to win the race. (not *hardly*)

Occasionally, for emphasis, it may be placed at the beginning of the sentence:

> Hard as he tried, he did not succeed.

But this is merely a stylistic device which varies the normal word order. The usual pattern is that given above.

N.B. To rain hard means ' to rain very heavily.'

Hardly means 'scarcely at all '. It is an adverb of degree, and is placed before the verb, or, in the case of compound tenses, between the first word of the auxiliary and the rest of the verb.

> He was so changed in appearance that I hardly knew him.
> She spoke so quietly that we could hardly hear her.
> This typewriter is as good as new; it has hardly been used.

Again, for emphasis it may be placed at the beginning of the sentence.

> Hardly had he recovered from one illness when he was stricken down by another.

Late (adverb) has two meanings.

1 ' After the time expected ' or ' after the time that one should have done (something) '.

> Every morning this week she has arrived late. (not *lately*)

2 ' Towards the end of a specified period of time'.

The robbery took place late at night.
He telephoned me late in the afternoon.
She did not marry until late in life.

Lately means more or less the same as *recently*.

Have you read any good novels lately?
I used to go to the cinema a good deal, but I have not been lately.

It differs from *recently*, however, in that it takes only a perfect tense, whereas *recently* may take either a perfect or a past.

I have not seen him recently.
He told me all the news when he visited me recently.

We can say *I have not seen him lately*, but not *I did not see him lately*.

Most (adverb) means ' to the greatest extent or degree '.

The food that I dislike most is cabbage. (not *mostly*)
The person who talks most is often the one who does least. (not *mostly*)

Mostly means ' for the most part '.

The audience consisted mostly of women.

EXERCISES

1 Fill in the blank spaces in the sentences below with *hard* or *hardly* (whichever you think correct).

a She has eaten ..... anything today.
b You will have to work ..... to pass your examination.
c He tried very ..... but did not succeed.
d We could ..... hear what the speaker said.
e The pupil strove ..... to get to the top of the class.
f We ..... ever see each other now.
g The child could ..... lift the heavy basket.
h We have been working ..... all day.
i It has been raining .....for the past two hours.
j He had ..... set foot on the street when he was knocked down by a car.

k The stranger looked ..... at me as he passed.
l The peasants had to work ..... for little reward.
m He has tried so ..... that he deserves praise.
n It was ..... light when we set out.
o The sick man could ..... speak, he was so weak.

2 Fill in the blank spaces in the following sentences with *late* or *lately*.

a How is your brother getting on? I have not seen him .....
b Peter arrived home very ..... last night.
c My birthday falls ..... in October.
d My sister has not been very well .....
e ..... the library has been used by fewer people.
f He missed his bus, and so got to work .....
g The fire broke out ..... on Saturday night.
h Have you had a letter from your cousin .....?
i Any one who comes ..... will have to sit at the back of the hall.
j The student worked ..... into the night.
k The train arrived ten minutes .....
l I have not been to the theatre .....
m The examination will take place ..... in March.
n We have not had very good weather .....
o The accident occurred ..... on Sunday evening.

3 Fill in each of the blank spaces in the following sentences with *most* or *mostly*.

a The books on the stall were ..... novels.
b It was John who helped me ...... to get over my difficulties.
c Of the three books, this is the one that interested me .....
d The great poets have been ..... men.
e Which of the subjects that you study do you care for .....?
f The prize should go, not necessarily to the person who succeeds, but to him who tries.....
g The trees in that plantation are..... birch.
h The students are ..... young people between the ages of sixteen and twenty.
i You should adopt the course which will benefit you .....
j The apples were ..... small ones.

4 Write three sentences of your own containing *hardly*, three containing *hard* (adverb), three containing *late* (adverb), three containing *lately*, three containing *most* (adverb) and three containing *mostly*.

8. *Fairly* and *rather*

Fairly is used only before positive adverbs and adjectives, and then only if they denote something which is considered desirable or is viewed with approval. It is not used of things which are undesirable or are viewed with disapproval.

Rather can be used for things either desirable or undesirable.

> The lecture was fairly interesting.
> The lecture was fairly well attended.
> The lecture was rather boring.
> The lecture was rather badly attended.

But not:

> The lecture was fairly boring.
> The lecture was fairly badly attended.

Rather is also used:

1 Before comparatives and before *too*. (Fairly cannot be used for either of these.)

> I am feeling rather better today. (But not *fairly better*)
> You read rather too quickly. (But not *fairly too quickly*)

2 Before certain nouns which are descriptive of an attitude towards a person or a thing.

> It is rather a pity to cut down those trees.
> She makes rather a fuss about trivial matters.
> He is rather a fool to give up a good job like that.

3 As an adverb of degree before verbs that express a feeling or an attitude of mind.

I rather like that picture.
I rather wish I had taken your advice.

EXERCISES

1 Insert *fairly* or *rather* in the following sentences.

a The patient is ..... better today.
b We have had a ..... good holiday.
c She can speak English ..... well.
d The price is ..... more than we wished to pay.
e We ..... hoped that you would join our party.
f She is ..... a silly kind of girl.
g This piece of work is ..... satisfactory.
h We found our way ..... easily.
i She reads ..... too quickly.
j I find this exercise ..... difficult.
k It was ..... stupid of you to say that.
l We have had ..... poor weather this summer.
m He is a ..... intelligent boy.
n We could understand what he said ..... well.
o This bread is ..... dry.
p We had a ..... comfortable journey.
q He is ..... a tyrant to those who work for him.
r It is ..... a shame to throw that book away.
s She can speak French ..... well, though she cannot read it.
t I ..... feared this would happen.

2 Compose sentences of your own in which the following words or expressions are used, preceded by *rather* or *fairly* (whichever you think suitable):

interesting; too big; easy; cheaper; too expensive; warm; deaf; lazy; well; more slowly; fast; tired; early; sooner; too heavy; a foolish person; light; foggy; tall; later; good; a clever girl; heavy; brave; too long

9. Adverbial use of *no, not* and *none*

1 When *no* is used before a positive adjective it is almost always itself an adjective, qualifying the same noun as the other adjective does. (For exceptions, see below, Note 1)

> They had no warm clothing. (i.e., no clothing that was warm)
> There are no stupid scholars in this class. (i.e., no scholars who are stupid)

2 It is also adjectival if it is used before a comparative adjective that is used attributively (i.e.. before a noun, to qualify it).

> There is no cleverer boy in the class than Tom. (i.e., no boy who is cleverer)

3 But if the attributive adjective, whether positive or comparative, is preceded by the indefinite article *a* or *an*, then *no* cannot be used. The verb must be made negative by the use of *not*.

> There is not a stupid scholar in the class.
> There is not a cleverer boy in the class than Tom.

4 *Not* is also used before a noun preceded by *a* or *an* even when it is not qualified by an adjective.

> Not a person could tell us the way.
> Not a morsel of food was wasted.

5 Adverbial *no* is used only (*a*) before comparative adverbs, (*b*) before comparative adjectives used as predicates.

> The bus will get you there no sooner than the train.
> He is no older than I am.
> This exercise is no better than the one you did before.

A positive adverb, or an adjective used predicatively, cannot be modified by *no*. *Not* must be used.

Incorrect	*Correct*
She is no very well today.	She is not very well today.
That clock is no right.	That clock is not right.

6 Adverbial *none* (not *no*) must be used before (*a*) *too* followed by a positive adjective or adverb, (*b*) *the* followed by a comparative adjective or adverb.

His health is none too good. (not *no too good*)
We arrived none too soon. (not *no too soon*)
We were none the worse for our experience. (not *no the worse*)

Notes

1. An exception to what has been said in **(5)** above is to be found in the sentence *This dress is no different from the other*, which is perfectly good English. Here we have a positive adjective modified by *no;* but it really goes with the comparatives, since the idea of difference implies comparison. And the same is true of *no other* in such a sentence as *We could be no other than pleased at the result.*

2. *No good*, in such a sentence as *It's no good doing that*, is an apparent exception, but not a real one, as *good* is here, historically, not an adjective but a noun, meaning 'advantage.' (It has the same meaning in *for the good of one's health.*) The pattern having become established, we then get such sentences as:

This medicine is no good.
He is no good at English.

These are quite correct, but *good* is still, historically, a noun, and *no* an adjective, though the original meaning has been completely lost.

3. Although *no* is used before *different*, it cannot be used before its opposite, *like*. Instead we must use *nothing*.

He is nothing like his brother.
This is nothing like Celia's writing.

EXERCISES

1 Insert *no* or *not* in the blank spaces in the following sentences.

a There was ..... a sound to be heard in the room.
b This work is ..... better than the previous piece was.
c We had ..... sooner set out than it started to rain.
d ..... a single person knew the answer.
e Can you think of ..... better reason than that?
f It is ..... warmer today than it was yesterday.
g It took us ..... less than three hours to do the work.
h ..... a star was to be seen in the sky.
i We ..... longer believe that madness is due to possession by evil spirits.
j ..... less than five people have tried to solve the problem. but ..... one of them has been able to do it.
k As they were ill they could ..... come to the party.
l You could make ..... greater mistake than that.
m The condition of the patient is ..... different today from what it was yesterday.
n There is ..... a cleverer girl in the school than Joan.
o ..... a spot of rain has fallen for over a month.
p It is ..... good wishing for the impossible.
q There is ..... the slightest truth in his story.
r The lecture was ..... very interesting.
s I can walk ..... faster than this.
t ..... a word was said about the theft of the diamonds.

2 Insert *no*, *none*, or *nothing* in the blank spaces in the following sentences.

a He explained the matter to us at great length, but we were ..... the wiser.
b It is ..... too warm today.
c An elephant is ..... like a giraffe.
d This cloth is ..... different from the other one.
e The police are ..... nearer a solution of the mystery than they were a week ago.
f The children were ..... the worse for their experience.
g The garden is still attractive, but it is ..... like it used to be.
h The pupils found the examination ..... too easy.

i He may be generous with his money, but I like him ..... the more for that.
j Will it be all right if we meet at six o'clock? Yes, but ..... later.

10. Difficulties with comparatives and superlatives

1 Some adjectives and adverbs are made comparative and superlative by adding *-er* and *-est* to the positive.

big, bigger, biggest; fast, faster, fastest; long, longer, longest.

Others use *more* and *most* before the positive.

beautiful, more beautiful, most beautiful; quickly, more quickly, most quickly.

It is never correct to use *more* and *most* as well as the suffix.

William is taller than John. (not *more taller*)
He is the tallest boy in the class. (not *the most tallest boy*)

2 When we compare two different things with a third, and wish to say that one of the two is superior to the third to an even greater degree than the other is, this is expressed by the comparative followed or preceded by *still*.

William is taller than John, but James is taller still. (not *more taller*)
A motor-car can go faster than a bicycle, but an aeroplane can travel still faster. (not *more faster*, or *more faster still*)

3 The word *than* must be preceded by a comparative adjective or adverb, never by a positive one, since *than* implies that two things are being compared, or that one is being compared with all the others of a certain type or group.

He receives a bigger salary than anyone else in the office.
They arrived sooner than we had expected.

This is also true of the expression *than ever*.

It is hotter than ever today. (not *hot than ever*)
The sun shone more brightly than ever. (not *brightly than ever*)

4 *Very* is followed by a positive adjective or adverb, but *much* always takes the comparative.

I am not feeling very well today. (not *much well*)
I am feeling much better today. (not *very better*)
I prefer thrillers to travel books, for they are so much more exciting. (Do not forget the *more*: not *so much exciting*)

Notes

1. An exception to the above rule is *different*. We can say that one thing is *not much different from another*, in spite of the fact that *different* is positive; but by its very nature, the word implies a comparison between two things. (See p. 38)

2. *It is not much good doing that* is quite correct English, but this does not violate the rule given above, since *good* is here, by origin, not an adjective, but a noun. (See p. 38)

3. Although *very* cannot be used before a comparative adjective, *very much* can. But then it is only *much* that modifies the comparative, and *very* in its turn modifies *much*.

My wife is very much better today.
It is not very much warmer today than it was yesterday.

5 A comparative adjective can be used only if *two* things are compared. If we compare or choose from amongst more than two, then we must use the superlative.

Geography is the most interesting of all the subjects I study. (not *the more interesting*)
Of the two languages I am learning, I find English the easier. (not *the easiest*)
Anne was the taller of the two girls. (not *the tallest*)

6 If we compare one thing with all others of its kind that we know or have experienced, then we are comparing amongst *many* things (i.e. more than two), and so we need a superlative. Consequently the following sentence is wrong:

This is a very interesting novel I have ever read.

It must be:

This is the most interesting novel I have ever read.

The following tables will give you the two possible patterns that can be used.

A

This is the most interesting novel	I have ever read.
That was the funniest story	I have ever heard.
Today is the warmest day	we have had this year.
He is the best actor	that has ever appeared on any stage.

B

Of all the novels I have read	this is the most interesting.
Of all the stories I have heard	that is the funniest.
Of my many friends	you are the one I value most.
Of the several methods we have tried	this is the easiest.

EXERCISES

1 Fill in the blank spaces in the following sentences with the comparative or the superlative degree, whichever you think is needed, of the adjective or adverb that is given in brackets at the end.

a This book is ..... than the other one was. (interesting)
b My grandmother is the ..... member of our family. (old)
c An aeroplane can travel ..... than a train. (fast)
d Everest is the ..... mountain in the world. (high)
e Who arrived ....., John or James? (early)

f This is the ..... piece of work I have ever undertaken. (difficult)
g She always did things the ..... way. (easy)
h Which season is ....., summer or winter? (hot)
i Who is the ..... pupil in your class? (tall)
j Which is the ..... way to the railway station? (near)
k Of the two brothers, the ..... was the ..... (young, clever)
l I shall not stay ..... than I can help. (long)
m The ..... I stay in this place, the ..... I like it. (long, much)
n Which of the three routes is the .....? (short)
o The ..... man that has ever lived could not answer that question. (wise)
p The carpet was ..... than we expected. (dear)
q The ..... person can sometimes make mistakes. (careful)
r Could you walk a little ..... please? (slow)
s That is the ..... joke I have ever heard. (good)
t The journey was the ..... we had ever experienced. (tedious)

2 Fill in the blank spaces in the sentences below with the correct form of the adjective or adverb given in brackets at the end.

a This box is ..... than the other one. (big)
b When my brother was at school he was the ..... boy in his class. (clever)
c That is the ..... story I have ever read. (thrilling)
d It is ..... today than it was yesterday, and tomorrow it will probably be ..... (hot)
e It is ..... to be healthy than to be ..... (good, rich)
f She is the ..... person I have ever met. (interesting)
g The..... we start, the ..... we shall get there. (soon)
h Haven't you a ..... hat than that? (good)
i Which of the three brothers is the ..... ? (young)
j A ..... name is ..... than gold. (good)
k I feel much ..... today than I did yesterday. (well)
l It is ..... than ever today. (cold)
m He is the ..... person in the village. (rich)
n You will have to do your work ..... than this. (carefully)
o There is no-one whom I esteem ..... than your father. (highly)

3 Fill in the blank spaces in the sentences below with *much* or *very* (whichever you think correct).

a You are ..... lucky to have escaped.
b This carpet is ..... better in quality than the other.
c She is not ..... older than I am.
d Is the message ..... urgent?
e My sister speaks English ..... well.
f She can speak it ..... better than I can.
g They should be here ..... soon.
h I hear that your mother has been ..... ill.
i Yes, she has, but she is ..... better now.
j The journey took us ..... longer, than we expected.
k We found the exhibition ..... interesting.
l I have ..... often wished I could visit Britain.
m Was your father ..... angry with you for staying out so late?
n Your friend is ..... late; we cannot wait for him ..... longer.
o After your explanation the subject is ..... clearer than it was before.

4 Fill in the first column of the following table with a suitable clause to go with that in the second column. The first one is done for you as an example. (*N.B.* The clause you insert must contain a superlative.)

Solomon was the wisest person	who has ever lived.
....	I have ever seen.
....	that you have done today.
....	that I have ever experienced.
....	we have played this season.
....	we have in the shop.

5 Fill in the second column of the table below with a suitable clause that goes with that in the first column. Again the first one is done as an example.

Solomon was the wisest person	*who has ever lived.*
That was the narrowest escape	....
This is the best car	....
That is the most difficult question	....
She is the most beautiful woman	....
This building is the highest	....

6 Insert in the blank spaces below the comparative or superlative degree of the word given in brackets at the end.

a Which of your sisters is ....., Jane or Mary? (old)
b Who is the ..... person in your family? (old)
c Which is the ..... day of the year? (long)
d That is the ..... valley I have ever seen. (beautiful)
e Which is the ....., iron or lead? (heavy)
f Is James or Henry the ..... of the two sons? (young)
g Both his children are clever, but the girl is the ..... of them. (clever)
h Which will get us there ....., the train or the bus? (quickly)
i This is by far the ..... of the two methods. (easy)
j Even the ..... person in the world could not solve that problem. (clever)

11. Confusion of participles: active and passive voice

1 With transitive verbs the present participle (the one ending in *-ing*) is active; it tells us something that a person or a thing does. The past participle is passive; it tells us something that is done to a person or a thing.

Burning wood = wood that is burning.
Burnt wood = wood that is or has been burnt.

A drying wind = a wind that dries things.
Dried fruit = fruit that has been dried.

2 If, therefore, we want, wish, require or should like something done *to* a person or a thing, we must use the past participle, not the present, to say what it is that is to be done.

I want this exercise *written* in ink. (not *writing*)
We should like the work *finished* by Friday. (not *finishing*)
Would you like the window *closed*? (not *closing*)

The verbs *need* and *want* can be followed by a verbal form ending in *-ing*. This, however, is the gerund, not the present participle. It is equivalent in meaning to a passive infinitive. Consequently the subject must denote the thing (or sometimes the person) that needs or wants something done to it.

> My shoes need mending.
> This dress wants washing.
> The invalid needs careful feeding.

3 The present participle can take only *be* as an auxiliary, never *have*.

> He *is* writing a book about his travels. (not *has writing*)
> The train *is* standing at the platform. (not *has standing*)

The past participle of transitive verbs can take both *be* and *have*. With *have* it makes an active voice, with *be* a passive.

> The sun *has* ripened the fruit. (active)
> The fruit *is* ripened by the sun. (passive)

The past participle of most intransitive verbs can take only *have*, since normally intransitive verbs are used only in the active voice.

> The girl *has* fainted. (not *is fainted*)
> My grandfather *has* died. (not *is died*)

There are a few, however, that can take both *have* and *be*, though with a slight difference of meaning.

> My father *has* gone to London.
> When he looked in the place where he had hidden the money, he found that it *was* gone.
> Mr Smith *has* retired from business.
> Mr Smith no longer goes to business; he *is* retired.

When it is preceded by the auxiliary *be*, the past participle of such verbs has the force of a predicative adjective describing a state, condition or situation.

4 Special care is necessary when the auxiliary is *have been has been* or *had been*. Because it starts with *have/has/had*, there is a temptation to regard it as a 'have' auxiliary, and to imagine that by placing the past participle after it, on the analogy of *I have finished my work*, we can make it active. But this is a mistake. *Have been* is a compound tense of the auxiliary *be*, not *have*. To become active it must therefore be followed by the present participle, and by the past participle to become passive.

Active Voice

I have not been waiting very long. (not *have not been waited*)
She had been visiting some friends. (not *had been visited*)
We have been playing cricket. (not *have been played*)

Passive Voice

All the food has been eaten. (not *eating*)
Our house has just been repainted. (not *repainting*)

5 There are some verbs which can be used either transitively or intransitively. In such cases *have/has/had been* can be followed only by the present participle for the intransitive use, but for the transitive by either the present or the past participle.

Intransitive

They have been working very hard today.

Transitive

You have been working that horse very hard.
That horse has been worked very hard.

6 The verbs *happen*, *occur*, *belong*, and *depend*[1] are never used in the passive.

The accident happened at 10 p.m. (not *was happened*)
The price depends on the quality. (not *is depended on*)
That car belongs to my father. (not *is belonged to*)
An explosion occurred in the factory. (not *was occurred*)

Similarly the compound verb *to take place* is intransitive in force, and can be used only in the active voice.

The wedding took place last Saturday. (not *was taken place*)

1. Except when *depend on* means more or less the same as *rely on*, and is preceded by *can* or *may*.
He is a person who can always be depended on.

7 The past participles of verbs denoting some kind of feeling or emotion can be used only of living creatures (usually only of human beings), and never of things, since things cannot experience feelings or emotions. Such verbs are *excite*, *interest*, *surprise*, *fascinate*, *frighten*, *satisfy*, to mention only a few.

She is interested in music.
We were surprised by the news.
They were fascinated by the conjurer's tricks.
The dog became very excited.
Are you satisfied with your new house?

The *present participle* of such verbs is used of the thing that provokes or gives rise to the feeling.

This book is very interesting.
They found the conjurer's tricks fascinating.
The film was most exciting.
I have just heard some surprising news.
The meal was quite satisfying.

EXERCISES

1 Fill in the blank spaces in the following sentences with the present or past participle (whichever you think correct) of the verb given in brackets at the end of the sentence.

a Two men were ..... in the doorway. (stand)
b Many houses were ..... by the gale. (damage)
c We have been ..... for over half an hour. (wait)
d The doctor has been ..... out to attend an urgent case. (call)
e I want these parcels ..... immediately. (deliver)
f Are you ..... the goods with you, or would you like them ..... on later? (take, send)
g She was ..... by the fire, ... a newspaper. (sit, read)
h This house has been ..... nearly a hundred years. (build)
i We should like two seats ..... for us. (reserve)
j They were ..... that their team had never been ..... (boast, beat)

2 Insert a tense of the verb *to be* or *to have* in the blank spaces in the following sentences.

a The little girl ..... crying because she ..... lost her money.
b My father ..... just bought a new car.
c When we set out it ..... raining very heavily.
d My aunt ..... coming to stay with us for a few days.
e I ..... misplaced my purse. ..... anyone seen it?
f He ..... crossing the road when he ..... knocked down by a cyclist.
g I ..... never been to Britain, but I ..... hoping to go there before long.
h Many accidents ..... been caused by careless driving.
i Who was that girl you ..... speaking to?
j On my twenty-first birthday I ..... given a gold watch as a present.
k Our team ..... been beaten only once this season.
l The thief ..... arrested by the police as he ..... leaving the railway station.
m ..... you heard the rumour that income tax ..... going to be reduced?
n My elder brother ..... studying for the legal profession.
o He ..... passed his first examination, and ..... taking the final examination next year.

3 In the blank spaces in the following sentences, insert the present or the past participle of the verb given in brackets at the end of the sentence.

a Are you ..... in stamp-collecting? (interest)
b It is ..... how soon the weather has changed. (surprise)
c The children were ..... at the prospect of going for a holiday. (excite)
d We were all ..... at the news of his success. (surprise)
e Our visitor had some ..... stories to tell about foreign parts. (interest)
f The skill of the conjuror was ..... (astonish)
g His audience was ..... at the tricks he performed. (astonish)
h That must have been a ..... experience. (terrify)
i The speaker held his audience ..... for over an hour. (interest)
j His friends were ..... by the news of his sudden death. (shock)

k It is a ..... state of affairs that people are allowed to starve while others live in luxury. (shock)
l A ..... face is a pleasure to behold. (smile)

4 Compose sentences of your own to illustrate the use of the following words:
amazing; terrifying; laughing; amused; interested; shocking; astonished; astonishing; pleasing; disappointed

12. The prop-word *one*

To avoid repeating a noun, we often use the word *one* (plural *ones*) to replace it.

We have sold our old car and bought a new one.

The following points should be noticed about the use of this word.

1 It can be used only for things that are countable (books, pens, desks, houses, cars, trains, toys, dogs, tables). It cannot be used for non-countables. We must say:

I prefer white coffee to black. (not *black one*)

2 It is always used:
(*a*) in conjunction with an adjective preceded by the indefinite article *a* or *an*, or by a possessive adjective (my, his, her, our, your, their).

We are moving from our present house into a smaller one. (not *into smaller one*)
Take off your blue dress and put on your green one. (not *put on green one*)

(*b*) with the definite article *the* preceding it, and an adjective phrase or adjective clause following it.

> If you can't find your pen, use the one on the table.
> Of the two watches, I prefer the one that you showed us first.

3 An exception to rule (*a*) above occurs with *this* and *that*, when the article *a* or *an* is never used.

> You sit in that chair, and I'll have this one.

This one and *that one* may, however, be followed by an adjective phrase or clause.

> The book I am referring to is that one on the second shelf.
> The most valuable ring that I possess is this one that I am wearing.

The article is not used, either, before *another one*; but then it is really already there, in the first syllable (*an-*) of *another*.

4 A plural noun is replaced by the plural *ones*.

> He ate all the big cherries and left me the little ones.

Even with things that are countable, *one/ones* cannot be used in the following cases.

(*a*) Immediately after a genitive or a possessive adjective, if no other adjective comes in between.

> As my own bicycle was broken, I borrowed John's. (not *John's one*)
> Is this my pen, or is it yours? (not *your one.*)

Note, incidentally, that the possessive adjective + *one/ones* is replaced by the possessive pronoun: *yours*, not *your; mine*, not *my*.

But we can say *John's old one*, *your new one*, *my best one*, because here another adjective comes between the possessive and the noun.

> You may borrow my old umbrella, if you wish, but I cannot lend you my best one.

(*b*) After *these* and *those*, in spite of the fact that it can be used after the singular *this* and *that*.

> I don't care for those flowers; I would rather have these. (not *these ones*)

(*c*) To replace class-nouns such as *furniture*, *luggage*, *cutlery* and *clothing*, which are countable things but are generalising terms and therefore express an idea which is itself non-countable.

> All the old knives have been replaced by new ones.

But:

> All the old cutlery has been replaced by new. (not *new one*, or *new ones*)

EXERCISES

1 In some of the blank spaces in the following sentences *one* or *ones* is required, in others it would be incorrect to use *one* or *ones*. Write out the sentences, either inserting the correct word, or leaving the sentence as it is, as the case may be. If you do not insert anything, no space should be left when you copy out the sentence.

a They have left their old house and gone into a bigger .....
b Mary has eaten all the big sweets, and left me the small ....
c My bicycle was more expensive than ..... (*your one* or *yours*)
d You sit on that seat and I'll sit on this .....
e My coat is almost worn out; I shall have to get a new .....
f Would you like these chocolates, or would you prefer those .....?
g I prefer China tea to Indian .....
h Take off those new shoes and put on your old .....
i Some people prefer brown bread, others prefer white .....
j If you can't get a brown loaf, get a white .....
k Your watch is a much better ..... than mine.
l The pupils write their exercises in black ink, but the teacher corrects them in red .....
m Joan was jealous because she thought her sister's present was better than ..... (*her one* or *hers*)
n Would you like these white flowers, or those red .....?
o As she hadn't a dictionary of her own, she borrowed her friend's .....

p Is that grey car .....? (*yours* or *your one*)
q The film we saw was an American .....
r If we can't find a hotel in this town, we will go on to the next .....
s If you could have your choice, would you rather have fair hair or dark .....?
t We failed to catch the train we had intended, so we had to go by a later .....

2 Include each of the following in a sentence of your own.

(*a*) a very long one, (*b*) all the broken ones, (*c*) a bigger one, (*d*) a very cheap one, (*e*) this one, (*f*) his black ones, (*g*) the most expensive one, (*h*) the best ones, (*i*) a strange one, (*j*) those tall ones.

3 Compose (*a*) five sentences of your own in which *one* is correctly used as a prop-word; (*b*) five in which *ones* is used; (*c*) five in which the genitive or a possessive adjective is correctly used with *one* or *ones.*

13. Prepositions

A. THE EXPRESSION OF TIME

1 *At* is used:

(*a*) For a certain moment or point in time.

We got up *at dawn* and had breakfast *at eight o'clock.*
The train leaves *at* 2.45 *p.m.*

(Similarly: at noon, at sunset, at midnight, at the end of the concert, at the beginning of the lesson)

(*b*) For festivals which mark a point in the year.

(Similarly: at the New Year, at the week-end, at dinner-time, at bed-time, at high tide, at low tide)

At is used for these because they are recurrent 'landmarks' in the speaker's reckoning of time, as the festivals are in the year.

2 *On* is used:

(*a*) For a specific day, whether it is given as a date (June 5th), as a day of the week (Wednesday), or as a special day in the year with a name of its own (New Year's Day, one's birthday, the anniversary of someone's death or of some happening).

I will come on Friday.
My sister was married on my sixteenth birthday.
She was born on August 15th, 1926.

(*b*) For a specific part of any such day (on the night of July 15th, on Friday afternoon, on Wednesday evening).

When we woke up on Friday morning it was raining.

3 *In* is used before words which denote a period of time. (in the summer, in September, in the year 1948, in the morning, in the evening, in the daytime, in the dinner-hour, in the English lesson, in the summer holidays)

We first came to live here in 1962.
Cricket is played in summer and football in winter.

In is also used:

(*a*) to show the total length of time taken for the completion of some activity or operation.

A good train will get you from Sheffield to London in three hours.
He ran the distance in three minutes, thirty-five seconds.

(*b*) to state a period at the end of which something will happen.

We shall be ready in a few minutes.
Come back in an hour's time.

4 *During* is used to express the idea:

(*a*) That an occurrence continues, or a situation persists, throughout the whole of a specified period.

During the war food was rationed.
We work during the day and sleep during the night.

(*b*) That an event took place, or is to take place, within a specified period of time. In this sense it means more or less the same as 'in the course of'.

The house was burgled during the night.
I will call to see you during the week.

5 *By* is used to denote the latest time by which something was or is to be done. The implication is that it may be done before then, but not after.

You must be home by ten o'clock.
The work should be finished by next Friday.
Applications for the post should be received by April 25th.

By is also used before the words *day* and *night* with practically the same meaning as 'during'.

Some motorists prefer to travel by night, when there is less traffic on the roads.
'The sun shall not smite thee by day, nor the moon by night.'

Similarly there is the phrase *by moonlight*.

'Look for me by moonlight, watch for me by moonlight; I'll come to thee by moonlight, though hell should bar the way.' (Alfred Noyes, *The Highwayman*)

6 *For* is used to show the lapse of time during which something takes place, or a state of affairs persists.

It rained continuously for twenty-four hours.
I have not seen him for a month.
We have been waiting for over an hour.
They will not be here for another two hours.

The difference between *We stayed a week* and *We stayed for a week* is that the former merely states the sum total of the time when it is reckoned up at the end of the stay, whereas the latter thinks of the time as it goes on, day by day, until a week has elapsed. Similarly compare:

She kept me talking half an hour.
She kept me talking for half an hour.
I can only stay a few minutes.
I can only stay for a few minutes.

Notes

1. The prepositions *at*, *on* and *in* are not used if the noun giving a time is preceded by an adjective.

I met him last Friday. (not *on last Friday*)
We are going away next week-end. (not *at next week-end*)
She will be eighteen next July. (not *in next July*)
The doctor calls to see him every day. (not *on every day*)

(Similarly: every morning, every night, every evening, every week, next week, next month, next year, next Monday, last week, last year, last month, a week next Monday, a fortnight next Friday, next Saturday evening, next Christmas, last Christmas)

But though we say *next Saturday*, if we reverse the order of the noun and adjective, we must use *on* (on Saturday next).

2. *Yesterday*, *today* and *tomorrow*, besides being nouns, are also used as adverbs, and therefore do not take a preposition.

I will telephone you tomorrow. (not *on tomorrow*)
Mary called to see me yesterday. (not *on yesterday*)
He promised to come today. (not *on today*)

(Similarly: yesterday evening, yesterday afternoon, a week ago yesterday, tomorrow morning, a week tomorrow, a fortnight today)

Though *yesterday* and *tomorrow* can both be followed by the words *morning*, *afternoon* and *evening*, *today* cannot. We must say *this morning*, *this afternoon*, and *this evening* (not *today morning*, etc.)

Night can be used only after *tomorrow*. We say *tomorrow night*, but not *yesterday night* or *today night*. Instead we say *last night* and *tonight* respectively.

EXERCISES

1 Fill in the blank spaces in the following sentences with the correct preposition.

a Shakespeare lived ..... the reigns of Elizabeth I and James I.
b He was born ..... 1564, and died ..... 1616.
c My birthday is ..... October 28th.
d The train leaves ..... 2.30, and arrives in Edinburgh ..... 6.15.
e I will call and see you ..... Sunday, ... three o'clock.
f The work must be finished ..... the end of the week.
g The burglars entered the house ..... the owner's absence.
h The exhibition is to be officially opened ..... Wednesday next, ... 3 p.m.
i Please let me have your answer ..... the end of the month at the latest.
j We are having a party ..... New Year's Day.
k She always went to see her parents ..... Christmas.
l A gale got up ..... the night, and did much damage.
m She will be twenty-five ..... August 11th.
n ..... what year was she born?
o I shall be back ..... about twenty minutes' time.
p Could you meet me ..... 2.30 ..... Saturday afternoon?
q They ought to be here ..... now.
r I will call at your office some time ..... the morning.
s They ceased work ..... sunset.
t Christmas Day is ..... December 25th.

2 In some of the blank spaces in the following sentences a preposition is needed, but in others it is not. Copy out the sentences, either inserting the correct preposition or leaving the sentence as it is. (If you insert no preposition, do not leave the space when you copy out the sentence.)

a I get up ..... seven o'clock every morning.
b It has been very warm ..... today, but it may be cooler ..... tomorrow.
c We leave for our holiday ..... Friday.
d The Second World War ended ..... 1945.
e Would it be convenient if I called to see you ..... one day.... next week?
f All the members of our family go to church ..... every Sunday. My sister and I usually go ..... the morning, but my mother and father go ..... the evening.
g ..... last week my grandparents celebrated the fiftieth anniversary of their wedding.
h I take up my new post ..... next April.
i We intend to go to the theatre ..... this evening. The performance begins ..... 7.30, so we ought to leave home .... seven o'clock at latest.
j A news bulletin is broadcast ..... six o'clock ..... each evening.
k .....one day you will regret what you have done.
l It has rained ..... every day ..... this week.
m My father will be retiring from business ..... two years' time.
n The subscription falls due ..... January 1st ..... each year.
o ..... ten o'clock only six people had arrived.

3 Make sentences of your own which include the following expressions used adverbially. Decide whether a preposition is required, and if it is, see that you use the correct one.

today; midnight; next year; every Saturday; eight o'clock; this afternoon; three months' time; last summer; the year 1805; each evening; many times

B. THE EXPRESSION OF PLACE

1 *Place of Residence* (*Countries, towns, etc.*)

(*a*) For the *kind* of place, when the reference is merely general and no specific place is named, use *in.*

> I like to spend the summer *in the country*, and the winter *in the town.*
> Many English people live *in cities.*

(Similarly: in a village, in the suburbs, in the desert: but *at* the seaside, and *on* an island)

(*b*) For the names of countries, continents, and large land areas such as counties, departments or provinces, and for capital cities or the names of large towns, use *in*.

We used to live in London/Kent/Alsace.
The Chinese live in China.
My married sister lives in Manchester.

(*c*) For villages and smaller towns, normally use *at*.

Mr Wickfield lived at Canterbury.
Shakespeare was born at Stratford-on-Avon.

But even in the case of a village or a small town, a speaker will use *in* when he identifies himself with the place, either because he lives there or because he happens to be there at the moment of speaking.

Have you lived in Cranford long? (not *at Cranford*)

2 *Places of Residence* (*Houses, etc.*)

(*a*) For the kind of house or residence, when no specific one is mentioned, use *in*.

She always thought she would like to live in a bungalow.

(Similarly: in a cottage, in a mansion, in a modern house, in a hotel, in a caravan, in a flat)

(*b*) For a particular house or place of residence, use *at*.

The Prime Minister lives at 10 Downing Street.

(Similarly: at Buckingham Palace, at The Rookery (the name of a house), at the Savoy Hotel)

(*c*) For the names of streets and roads, use *in*.

Sherlock Holmes lived in Baker Street.

3 *Places of Work*

(*a*) For the kind of place, use *in* if it is a building.

His father works in a bank.

(Similarly: in an office, in a shop, in a factory, in a restaurant)

But if it is not a building, use *on*: on a farm, on the railway, on an estate, on a rubber plantation.

(*b*) If a particular place is indicated, *at* is generally used.

Both my brothers work at the Town Hall.

(Similarly: at the Public Library, at the railway station, at Gamages, at Hudson's Restaurant, at the City General Hospital, at the Atomic Research Establishment)

(*c*) For a particular room or department, use *in*.

He is employed in the Manuscripts Department at the British Museum.

(Similarly: in the Cataloguing Department of the Public Library, in the Furnishing Department of Gamages.)

EXERCISES

Supply the correct preposition in the following sentences.

1. Would you rather live ..... the town, or ..... the country?
2. My uncle lives ..... a large house ..... a village a few miles from Rouen.
3. John was brought up ..... a farm, but at the age of sixteen he was sent to work ..... a shop ..... a neighbouring town.
4. My father is employed as a cashier ..... the local branch of the Midland Bank.
5. When we were ..... London we stayed ..... the Cumberland Hotel.
6. He told me that he lived ..... 23 Clarendon Road.
7. When he retired, he left London and went to live ..... Kent.
8. People who live ..... glass houses should not throw stones.
9. Mr Smith teaches Modern Languages ..... the High School.
10. I believe his father is a solicitor ..... a small town not far from here.
11. He gave us to understand that he had some sort of job ..... the dockyard.
12. A friend of my father's has offered to get me a post ..... the office ..... a large steel works.
13. Miss Johnson is a typist ..... the Town Hall.
14. Would you prefer to work ..... a factory, or ..... a farm?
15. Mr and Mrs Jones stay ..... the seaside for a month each year.

C. PREPOSITIONS ATTACHED TO VERBS

1 *The error of omitting the preposition*

A number of English verbs which are intransitive, and which

therefore cannot take an object of their own, are followed by a preposition and its object. The preposition must not be omitted, otherwise the sentence will be incorrect.

Do not say,

He pointed the tree.

Say,

He pointed *to* the tree.
He pointed *at* the tree.
He pointed *out*[1] the tree.

Do not say,

We listened the music.

Say,

We listened *to* the music.

Do not say,

I am looking a book.

Say,

I am looking *for* a book. or I am looking *at* a book.

There are so many of these verbs that it would be impossible to give a complete list, but the following are a few that the student may find it useful to remember.

I do not agree *with*	what you say.
I am willing to agree *to*	your suggestion.
You should apply *for*	that post.
For information you should apply *to*	the secretary.
The regulations apply *to*	all office workers.
When shall we arrive *at*	our destination?
You must attend *to*	his instructions.
We had to compete *against*	a much stronger team.
I cannot hope to compete *with*	so experienced a player.
My sister does not care *for*	rice pudding.
Doctors and nurses care *for*	the sick.
One should always defer *to*	one's elders.
The train will depart *from*	the other platform.
Many people were gazing *at*	the spectacle.
We hope *for*	an easy examination.

[1] Here *out* is not a preposition, but an adverb, but it is included along with the other examples as the same mistake is sometimes made.

I insist *on*	accuracy in your work.
We all listened *to*	his story.
The servant was told to listen *for*	the door bell.
The pupils longed *for*	the end of the lesson.
The teacher was looking *for*	a piece of chalk.
She spends hours looking *at*	pictures.
Do you object *to*	my opening the window?
The girl pointed *to*	a stain on her coat.
The teacher pointed *out*	the pupil's mistakes.
It is rude to point *at*	people.
I rely *on*	his help.
I wish to remind you *of*	the promise you made.
One day you will repent *of*	what you have done.
I must reply *to*	his letter.
The price depends *on*	the quality.
Could I please speak *to*	the manager?
He refused to speak *of* (or *about*)	his achievements.
Everyone stared *at*	the newcomer.
Every ambitious person strives *for*	promotion.
I hope you succeed *in*	your task.
We all sympathise *with*	the unfortunate person.
My brother talks *of*	emigrating to Canada.
I wish you would not talk *about*	such painful things.
I cannot think *of*	his name.
What did you think *of*	that film?
I will think *about*	the matter.
We could not wish *for*	better weather than this.
Every week I write *to*	my aunt.

When these verbs and others like them are used in sentences which begin with an interrogative word like *what?*, *which?*, *who?*, *where?*, care must be taken not to omit the preposition, which then goes at the end, immediately after the verb.

What are you looking at? (not *What are you looking?*)
What is the teacher looking for? (not *What is the teacher looking?*)
Who was he pointing at? (not *Who was he pointing?*)
Where has this bus come from? (not *Where has this bus come?*)

Whom do you wish to speak to? (not *Whom do you wish to speak?*)

It will be noticed that the verb which precedes the preposition in all the above examples is an intransitive one; but in many cases the two words (verb+preposition) taken together have the force of a single transitive verb. In such cases a passive use is possible.

His hat *was sat on* by a very fat man.
No-one likes *being stared at.*
The children *were looked after* by their aunt.

EXERCISES

1 Give the questions to which the following statements might be the answers. Use such interrogative words as *who?*, *which?*, *what?*, *where?* to introduce the question, e.g. *This train has come from Edinburgh.—Where has this train come from?*

a I am looking for an English dictionary.
b Everyone was talking about the latest news.
c I was speaking to a friend.
d He was sitting in that chair.
e Mr Smith lives in that house.
f I am writing to my mother.
g Everyone was staring at the strange-looking person.
h We are listening to the music.
i I shall come by the train that leaves here at 3.30.
j I am thinking about that holiday I had in Paris.
k That box is made of wood.
l I gave the book to my sister.
m The train starts from platform number 5.
n I am waiting for a friend whom I have arranged to meet.
o He borrowed the book from a friend.

2 Complete the unfinished sentences in the following groups by using the same verb (though any tense of it you think suitable) that is used in the first sentence of each group.

a She is looking at a picture.
What is she .....?
In the museum there are all kinds of things to .....

b He stood on a chair to reach the top shelf.
What did he .....?
In order to reach the top shelf I need something to .....
Why are you..... that chair?

c John is waiting for his friend.
Who is John .....?
I shall not ..... him any longer.

d We have been talking about the film we saw last evening.
What are you .....?
Have you nothing better to ..... than that?
Some people are always ..... their illnesses.

e We offered to look after the children while their mother went to the shop.
The sick woman had no-one to ..... her.
She thanked me for ..... her dog while she was away from home.

f The bank manager lives in a large house.
What kind of a house do you .....?
After the hurricane many families had no house to .....

g The bill for the goods came to ten shillings.
How much does the bill .....?
If you let me know how much the bill ....., I will pay it.

h The goods were packed in a cardboard box.
What were the goods .....?
I want something to ..... these goods .....

3 Make up sentences of your own containing the following expressions. You may use any tense of the verb.

run after; fall over; look for; think of; speak to; play with; write to; laugh at; go to; attend to

4 In each of the following sentences a combination of a verb and a preposition is printed in italics. Write another sentence of your own using this same combination (any tense of it) in the passive voice. Here is one done for you, to give you the idea.

Who was that person that *spoke to* you?

Passive. You should not speak unless you are spoken to.

a I cannot *think of* his name.
b What are you *looking at*?

c Do not *interfere with* that machine.
d We *have paid for* everything we have bought.
e The cyclist *ran over* a child.
f You should *attend to* your lessons.
g The secretary *has written to* all the members.
h The child's parents let him have everything he *asked for.*
i If you are ill, you should *send for* the doctor.
j I have never *heard of* such a thing.

2. *Mistaken use of a preposition where none is required*

There are certain verbs which are transitive in English, though their equivalents in some other languages are followed by a preposition. The most frequently used are the verbs *answer*, *approach*, *ask*, *attack*, *enter* (when it means 'go in') and *resemble*. The foreign student of English must remember that, apart from the exceptions given in the notes at the end of the present section, a preposition is *not* used after these verbs. The following examples show the correct use, and warn against the incorrect.

CORRECT	*INCORRECT*
He refused to answer me.	He refused to answer *to* me.
I could not answer the question.	I could not answer *to* the question.
We approached the house.	We approached *to* the house.
I asked him a question.	I asked a question *to* him.
They attacked the town.	They attacked *against* the town.
The dog attacked the child.	The dog attacked *against* the child.
We entered the room.	We entered *into* the room.
The animal resembled a rat.	The animal resembled *to* a rat.

Notes

1. *Answer to* is used when the meaning is 'correspond with'.

There was no-one in the room who answered to the description of the person I was looking for.

2. *Enter into* is used when the meaning is 'embark upon' 'take part in' or 'consider'.

We cannot enter into a discussion of the matter now.
Our companions soon entered into the spirit of the game.
If you enter into an agreement, you should honour it.

Enter into, in the sense of 'go in' is often used in the Authorised Version of the Bible (1611), but it is now archaic.

EXERCISES

Complete the following sentences by using the verb given in brackets at the end, either with or without a preposition (whichever you think is correct).

1. As I ..... him he turned and walked away. (approach)
2. We saw two women ..... the shop. (enter)
3. The child ..... its father in looks. (resemble)
4. He gave us a general description of the plan, but did not ..... details. (enter)
5. The ruffian ..... the traveller with a stout stick. (attack)
6. We could find no-one who could ..... our inquiries. (answer)
7. She addressed me so rudely that I refused to ..... her. (answer)
8. The policeman ..... the motorist to move his car, as it was obstructing the traffic. (ask)
9. You need not ..... the question if you do not wish. (answer)
10. The teacher invited each of the pupils to ..... him a question in English. (ask)
11. The contents of the package did not ..... the details given in the list that accompanied it. (answer)
12. As we ..... the town the traffic became denser. (approach)
13. You should not ..... your aunt in that rude manner. (answer)
14. In shape, the object ..... an egg. (resemble)
15. The enemy ..... the fortress three times, but all in vain. (attack)
16. I recognised him as soon as he .....the room. (enter)
17. The police would not allow anyone to ..... the building. (enter)
18. Have you ..... his letter yet? (answer)
19. If you ..... that dog, it may ..... you. (approach, attack)
20. If you do not know the way, ... someone who does. (ask)

D. THE IDIOMATIC USE OF PREPOSITIONS

Below are some of the commoner expressions in English which involve the use of a preposition. Others will be found on pages 61 and 124. Note the correct preposition to use.

ACCUSE He accused me *of* cheating him. (not *for*)
The prisoner was accused *of* murder.

AFRAID My small sister is afraid *of* dogs. (not *from*)
She hesitated to cross the road, as she was afraid *of* being knocked down by a car.

When *afraid* is followed by an infinitive, no preposition is used. (See p. 124)

She was afraid to go near the fierce-looking dog.

ANGRY The father was very angry *with* his son. (not *at* or *against*)

But: I was very angry *at* what he said.

We are angry *with* a person, but *at* something he does or says.

APPROVE I do not approve *of* your action.

ARRIVE I usually arrive *at* school about ten minutes to nine. (not *arrive to school*)

When *arrive* is followed by an adverb of place such as *here*, *there*, *somewhere*, *anywhere*, *nowhere*, no preposition is used. *Home* is such an adverb, and therefore is not preceded by a preposition.

Has your father arrived home yet? (not *at home*, or *to home*)

But if *home* is preceded by a genitive or a possessive adjective, then it is a noun, and must take the preposition.

It was almost two o'clock when we arrived *at* my friend's home.

BOAST A modest person does not boast *of* his achievements. (not *for* or *at*)

Boast about is also correct.

He is not the kind of person to boast about his achievements.

CAREFUL She is very careful *of* her health. (not *for*).

When it is followed by an infinitive, *careful* takes no preposition.

Be careful not to spill the liquid.

He was very careful to see that everything was locked up before he left the office.

CARELESS He drove at a reckless speed, quite careless *of* the danger to himself and to others.

CURE This mixture is guaranteed to cure you *of* influenza in twenty-four hours. (not *from*)

He was quickly cured *of* his cold.

But when *cure* is a noun (meaning 'a remedy'), the preposition is *for*.

What is the best cure *for* a cold?

DIE People die *of* a disease or illness, but *from* doing something.

Many people have died *of* malaria.

He died *from* over-eating.

DIFFERENT This is different *from* the other. (not *to* or *than*)

The verb *differ* also takes *from*.

How does this differ *from* the other?

DISAPPROVE I disapprove *of* your conduct. (not *with* or *about*)

DRESS(ED) My sister always dresses *in* bright colours. (not *with*)

The lady was dressed *in* black.

FULL The chest was full *of* papers. (not *with*)

But we say 'full up *with*.'

GLAD We were very glad *of* a rest after our long journey. (not *for*)

But no preposition is used when *glad* is followed by an infinitive.

We were glad to be home again.

HELPFUL Your suggestion was very helpful *to* us. (not *for*)

INTERESTED She is very interested *in* stamp-collecting. (not *with*)

We are not interested *in* your story.

But when *interested* is part of a passive voice, then the preposition is *by*.

We were interested *by* what he had to say.

LIVE His wages are so small that he can scarcely live *on* them. (not *with* or *by*)

He earns scarcely enough to live *on*.

Cows live *on* grass.

But when *live* means ' to earn a living ', then *by* is used to specify the means or method.

He lived *by* cheating others.

MAKE Flour is made *from* wheat. (not *of*)

(MADE) Her dress was made *of* silk. (not *from*)

When one substance is changed into another, so that a new substance is produced, we use *from*, but when the original material is not actually changed, but is merely formed into some object, then we use *of*.

MARRIED When *married* is a verb it may be used either intransitively or transitively. In the latter case, no preposition is needed.

He married when he was twenty-seven.

He married my sister. (not *to my sister*)

When it is an adjective used predicatively, the preposition *to* is used.

He is married *to* my sister.

PLEASED The teacher was very pleased *with* the boy's progress. (not *for*)

The little girl was pleased *with* her new dress.

When *pleased* is followed by an infinitive, no preposition is used.

We were pleased to hear that he had recovered *from* his illness.

Again, no preposition is used before a clause.

We are pleased that you have been able to come.

PREFER I prefer a humorous play *to* a serious one. (not *than*)

PROUD We are proud *of* our new car.
She was very proud *of* her son's achievement. (not *for*)

RID Whether *rid* is used as a verb or as an adjective, it is followed by *of*.

The Pied Piper of Hamelin promised to rid the town *of* rats. (not *from*)
They were pleased to be rid *of* such a rogue. (not *from*)
I cannot get rid *of* my cold.

SIT A person sits *at* a desk, *on* a chair or a seat (but *in* an armchair), *in* a car, *in* a room.

The pupils were sitting *at* their desks.
There is no chair for me to sit *on*.
Let us sit *on* this seat for a while.
The old lady was sitting *in* an armchair.
While Mr Smith went in the shop, his wife sat *in* the car.

We sit *at* something that is placed before us, *on* something that is beneath us and *in* something that is around us or to some extent encloses us.

Sit *in* your places.
While we were sitting *at* dinner we heard a disturbance outside.

SORRY We were all sorry *for* the unfortunate person.
We are sorry *about* your misfortune.

We are sorry *for* a person, but *about* something that has happened. We may sometimes say, in conversation, *I am sorry about your mother*, but this really means about something that has happened to your mother. (She is ill, has had an accident, has died).

No preposition is used when *sorry* is followed by an infinitive.

We are sorry to hear that you have not been well.
I am sorry to say that he did not keep his word.

TAKE CARE You should take care *of* your health. (not *for*)
Will you take care *of* our dog while we are away from home?

No preposition is used before an infinitive or a clause.

Take care to lock everything up safely.
I'll take care that this does not happen again.

USEFUL This will be very useful *to* me.
A map is useful *for* finding one's way about.

Useful *to* a person, but *for* a purpose. The same distinction applies to:

USELESS This tool is quite useless *to* me.
This tool is quite useless *for* my purpose.
A small saw is useless *for* cutting down trees.

As can also be used when the meaning is 'in the capacity of'.
This substance is useless *as* a substitute for leather.

WRITE The note was written *in* pencil/*in* ink. (not *with*)
Write the exercise *in* ink. (not *with ink*)

But:
The note was written *with a* pencil/*with a* pen.

When *written* refers merely to the appearance of the words or the letters on the paper, then *in* is used; but when *was written* is a verb in the passive voice, and refers to the act of writing itself, and the thing named is the instrument used, then the correct preposition is *with*.

I cannot write *with* this pen.
She writes *with* her left hand.

EXERCISES

Complete the following sentences by adding the correct preposition in the blank spaces.

1. Your father will be very angry ..... you when he hears of your conduct.
2. She found a purse full ..... money.
3. No-one has yet discovered a cure ..... the common cold.
4. As we had had no food for over six hours we were glad ..... a meal.
5. Are you interested ..... modern art?
6. I prefer coffee..... tea.
7. I feel sorry..... Mrs Smith; two of her children are ill and her husband is unemployed.
8. The great English poet John Keats died ..... consumption.
9. We were glad to get rid ..... such an untrustworthy person.
10. He accused one of his friends ..... stealing his watch.
11. What time did you arrive ..... the office this morning?

12. Our parents did not approve ..... playing games on Sunday.
13. We are sorry ..... your mother's illness.
14. This coat should last you a long time if you take care ..... it.
15. As all the chairs were full, we had to sit ..... the floor.
16. She always dresses ..... bright colours.
17. His signature was written ..... pencil.
18. You had better tell the police what you have heard; it may be useful ..... them.
19. Which hand do you write ..... ?
20. Don't throw that piece of rag away; it may be useful ..... polishing the car.
21. Her shoes were made ..... the finest leather.
22. We are very pleased ..... our new house.
23. That small boy is very proud ..... his father.
24. Some women are afraid ..... mice.
25. He sat ..... the table writing a letter.
26. Ever since her early years she had lived .... the best of food.
27. That poor old lady must find it difficult to live ..... her small income.
28. The teacher was very angry ..... what had occurred in the classroom.
29. This drink is made ..... fresh fruit and sugar.
30. The prisoner was accused ..... ill-treating his small child.

14. The word *home:* used with and without a preposition

1 After such verbs as *come*, *go*, *arrive*, *get*, *send*, *take*, *bring*, where it indicates destination, the word *home* is an adverb, and therefore no preposition is used before it.

> Father comes home at five o'clock. (not *to home* or *at home*)
> We hope to arrive home about 8.30. (not *to home* or *at home*)

The children brought a stray kitten home.

But if *home* is preceded by a genitive or a possessive adjective, then it is a noun, and a preposition is necessary in order to make an adverb or adjective phrase. After *come*, *go*, *get*, *send*, *take* and *bring*, the preposition used is *to;* after *arrive* it is *at*.

I arranged to go to my friend's home for tea.
We could get to your home by six o'clock, if that would be convenient.

No preposition is used after *reach*, since *reach* is a transitive verb, and *home* is its object. The same applies to *leave*.

We hope to reach home by about 7.30.
What is the best way to reach your home?
We left home at 11.30.

2 If *home* represents the place where one is, or where one does something, then it must be preceded by the preposition *at*.

Mr Smith is not at home.
If you are not well, you should stay at home.

(Similarly: live at home, work at home, dine at home)

The following sentence, in which both *home* and *at home* are used, will illustrate the difference between the two.

Mr Smith is not *at home*; he will not be *home* until six o'clock.

The first part of the sentence means that Mr Smith is not in the house. The second part means that he will not have returned from work, or from a journey, until six o'clock.

EXERCISES

1 Insert *home* or *at home* (whichever you think is correct) in the blank spaces in the following sentences.

a Has your father come ..... from work yet?
b What time do you get ..... from the office?
c We are spending our holidays ..... this year.
d Susan has brought a friend ..... to tea.
e I am afraid you cannot see Mrs Smith, as she is not .....
f I could not unlock my desk, as I had left my keys .....
g I leave .... every morning at eight o'clock.

h I will telephone you as soon as I arrive .....
i Janet is married and has a house in the country, but Mary lives ..... with her parents.
j We called at the house, but there was no-one .....
k If the train is punctual, we should reach ..... about six o'clock.
l I shall go ..... as soon as I have finished my work.

2 Compose five sentences of your own using *at home*, and five using *home* as an adverb, without a preposition before it.

3 Fill in the blank spaces in the following sentences with *home*, or with *home* preceded by a preposition (whichever you think is required). If a preposition is needed, make sure you use the right one.

a She spent the afternoon ..... her friend's .....
b We are not far .... now.
c We were glad to get .... after our long journey.
d Some children go ..... for their midday meal; others have it at school.
e I don't think there is anyone ..... in that house.
f She arrived ..... heavily laden with purchases from her afternoon's shopping.
g The police called ..... the ..... of each of the suspected persons.
h He travels ..... his ..... to the office by car each day.
i The boy took the stray dog ..... his .....
j Would you care to come ..... to tea with me?
k They ran all the way .....
l When they got to the house they found no-one.....
m When he arrived at school he found he had left his book .....
n If it is fine I usually walk .... from work.
o The doctor went ..... the patient's ..... as soon as he received the message.
p We have had an enjoyable holiday, but it is pleasant to be .....again.
q As the pupil was not well the teacher sent him .....
r They returned ..... sooner than was expected.
s As she was ill and could not come out we went to visit her ..... her .....
t Need you go ..... yet?

15. Negative verbs

To make a verb negative, the word *not* is used. Take care to place it in the right position and to use the correct form of the verb with it.

1 In statements, if the positive verb is a simple tense form (I like, he eats, they ate), use *do* or *did* and the infinitive without *to*, and put *not* between the two words.

I like chocolates.
I *do not like* chocolates.
A cow eats grass.
A vegetarian *does not eat* meat.
The children ate their dinner.
The children *did not eat* their dinner. (not *did not ate*)

There are two exceptions to this rule.

(*a*) For the verb *to be* merely put *not* after the positive verb form.

This room is very warm.
This room *is not* very warm.
The exercises were difficult.
The exercises *were not* difficult.

(*b*) For *have*, when it is an auxiliary or when it shows possession or some idea closely related to possession, do not use the *do* forms; merely put *not* after the positive verb.

I *have not* seen him for about six months.
He *has not* the ability to do the work.
They *had not* the faintest idea where they were.

In spoken English and also in written English of the less formal kind, *have not*, *has not*, and *had not* are usually contracted to *haven't*, *hasn't* and *hadn't* respectively.

I haven't seen him for about six months.
He hasn't the ability to do the work.
They hadn't the faintest idea where they were.

When *have* expresses some other idea than possession, however, it follows the pattern of other regular verbs, and uses *do* in the negative.

I don't have indigestion any longer. (i.e. suffer from)
We didn't have any breakfast this morning. (i.e. partake of)

A more detailed treatment of this point will be found on pages 167–9.

When the positive verb is a compound tense form, it remains unchanged for the negative, and *not* is placed after the first auxiliary.

He has eaten his dinner.
He *has not eaten* his dinner.
The driver of the car was injured.
The driver of the car *was not injured.*
Those exercises have been marked.
Those exercises *have not been marked.*
I shall go to the meeting.
I *shall not go* to the meeting.

Can, *may*, *must*, *ought* and *need*, are treated as auxiliaries, and *not* is placed immediately after them.

I *cannot* hear what you say.
You *must not* do that.
We *need not* start yet.
He *may not* be able to come.
You *ought not* to waste your time.

Notes

1. *Cannot* is written as one word, but *could not* is always two, unless it is contracted to *couldn't*.

2. The contracted forms are generally used in spoken English. They are as follows.

is not—isn't	cannot—can't
I am not—I'm not	could not—couldn't
are not—aren't	must not—mustn't
was not—wasn't	need not—needn't
were not—weren't	ought not—oughtn't
do not—don't	shall not—shan't
does not—doesn't	will not—won't
did not—didn't	should not—shouldn't
	would not—wouldn't

The contracted forms *mayn't* and *mightn't* are sometimes heard in speech, but they are usually avoided, as they are awkward to pronounce.

2 For questions, the same verb form is used as for the corresponding negative statement, but the subject is placed after *not*, and the contracted forms of the negative verbs are normally used.

He does not eat meat.	They haven't any money.
Doesn't he eat meat?	Haven't they any money?
I have not seen him.	My mother is not well.
Haven't you seen him?	Isn't your mother well?

It is not impossible to say, *Is your mother not well*? and *Does he not eat meat*?, but it is rather formal, and sometimes conveys a slightly different shade of meaning from the ordinary contracted form.

The interrogative form of *I am not* is *aren't I*? (colloquial) or *am I not*? (more formal).

Am I not good enough for you to associate with?
Aren't I good enough for you to associate with?

3 For a negative imperative, the *do* form of the verb is used, with *not* following *do*.

Open the window.
Do not open the window. (Or, in spoken English, *Don't open the window*.)
(Similarly: Don't tease the cat. Don't take any risks. Don't be late for dinner.)

Older English often used the simple positive imperative followed by *not* but this is now confined to poetry:

'*Say not* the struggle naught availeth.'
'*Be not* anxious for the morrow.'

4 To make an infinitive negative, *not* must be placed before the *to*.

I told him *not to do it.*
We tried *not to laugh.*
She asked us *not to be late.*

(It would be incorrect to say *to not do it*, *to not laugh* and *to not be late.*)

EXERCISES

1 Write the following sentences in the negative form.

a We are hungry.
b The policeman caught the thief.
c It has been raining very heavily.
d Are you Mr Brown?
e The car was badly damaged.
f My father can speak Russian.
g I found that book very interesting.
h We ought to hurry.
i Will you have another cup of tea?
j Close the door, please.
k We have a television set.
l I shall buy a new hat next week.
m Are you well?
n The prisoner managed to escape.
o Your aunt has arrived.

2 Give a negative reply to the following questions.

a Is it time for lunch yet?
b Is he seriously ill?
c Did the explosion do much damage?
d Have you ever been to Britain?
e Have you any brothers?
f Did you hear what he said?
g Can you read the address on this letter?
h Need we pay the bill this week?
i Has the doctor been yet?
j Ought I to give the porter a tip?

3 Turn the following negative statements into negative questions, e.g. John does not like English grammar.—Doesn't John like English grammar?

a His father is not still living.
b I cannot drink this coffee.
c This book is not very easy to read.
d Her parents were not cross with her.
e I haven't any money.
f George will not lend us his camera.
g My sister has not finished her homework yet.
h The conductor would not let them get on the bus.
i He is not sixteen yet.
j They did not care for the concert.

4 Sometimes, instead of making a positive statement, English speakers use a negative question: e.g., instead of *It is cold today* they say *Isn't it cold today?* Such questions are felt to be more expressive of feeling than the corresponding statement would be. Although they appear to ask for the opinion of the person addressed, they really express the opinion of the speaker, with which it is assumed the other person will agree.

Express the following statements in the form of negative questions.

a That girl is tall.
b Her dress looks pretty.
c That man has a gruff voice.
d The car swerved as it rounded the corner.
e Mary likes ice-cream.
f Those boys were rude to that elderly gentleman.
g I told you you weren't to play near the pond.
h Your parents will be pleased when they hear of your success.
i I am clever, to answer such a difficult question as that.
j She screeches when she sings.
k It was dark in the cave.
l There was a strong wind last night.
m Harry would have loved to see this view.
n He is stupid, to waste his money like that.
o We had an enjoyable holiday.

16. Tenses

A. SIMPLE AND PROGRESSIVE (CONTINUOUS) FORMS OF THE PRESENT TENSE

1 The following rule holds good for most English verbs. There are some exceptions to it, notably the verb *to have* when it denotes possession or ownership, but these exceptions may be disregarded for the time being.

The simple form of the present tense (he moves, it falls, I come, we drink) is used to express:

(*a*) What is stated as always true, in the nature of things.

The earth *moves* round the sun.
Rain *falls* from the clouds.
Death *comes* to everyone sooner or later.
We *see* with our eyes, *hear* with our ears, and *smell* with our nose.

(*b*) What is habitual or recurrent.

I *come* to school by bus.
I *drink* tea, but my sister *prefers* coffee.
The shop *opens* at nine o'clock each morning.

2 To express a specific activity that is happening at the time of speaking, and is not yet completed, the progressive (or continuous) form of the present tense is used. This is formed by the present participle of the verb in question, preceded by the present tense of the verb *to be* as an auxiliary.

The clouds *are moving* across the sky.
The bus *is coming* round the corner.
The cat *is drinking* the milk.

3 Where a situation rather than an activity is concerned, if the situation is temporary only, the progressive form is used.

Jack *is standing* by the fire.
The washing *is hanging* on the line.

But for a situation or a fact that is permanent, the simple form is used.

> London *stands* on the Thames. (not *is standing*)
> My house *faces* south. (not *is facing*)
> This road *runs* from London to Dover. (not *is running*)

The same applies in interrogative sentences, but the simple form is rendered by *do* followed by an infinitive without *to*.

> Do you drink coffee?
> Does your house face south?

The progressive form is given by *be*+subject+present participle.

> Are you drinking coffee?
> Is Jack standing by the fire?

4 As exceptions to, or modifications of, what has been said above, the following should be noted.

(*a*) The simple form is used, even for something that is still in progress, if the sentence begins with a demonstrative *here* or *there*. The chief verbs thus affected are *come* and *go*.

Here comes the bride.	(not *Here is coming*)
There goes the bus.	(not *There is going*)
Here they come.	(not *Here they are coming*)
There she blows!	(not *There she is blowing*)

(*b*) Verbs denoting perception by one of the physical senses (see, hear, smell, feel, taste) do not use the progressive form to express an experience on a specific occasion, or one that is in progress. The simple form is sometimes used.

> I smell something burning.
> I see a train coming.

But the more usual construction is can+the infinitive.

> I can smell something burning.
> I can see a train coming.
> I can hear a dog barking.

When the progressive form is used, it refers to something that is continuous over a much longer period.

I am hearing much better since I had that operation.

N.B. Some of these verbs are also used with other meanings, and then they follow the normal patterns.

You're seeing things. (i.e., suffering from hallucinations)
He was smelling at the bottle (i.e., sniffing), to try and find out what had been in it.

(*c*) *Feel*, when it means ' experience a sensation ' (feel cold, feel sick, feel ill, feel better, feel sad), and *think* when it means ' be of the opinion ', normally use the simple form of the present even for a specific occasion.

I feel tired. I feel sick. I feel better today.
I think you are wrong.

The progressive is possible, though it usually suggests that the state is temporary.

I am feeling tired. I am feeling hungry.
I did not feel very well yesterday, but I am feeling better today.

(*d*) Certain situations which are more or less permanent (see section **3** above) may sometimes be presented by a speaker or writer as though they were temporary, because he is thinking of them only from the point of view of the moment when he saw them. In that case the progressive form of the verb may be used.

The house is facing south.
You can't miss the church; its spire is towering above the other buildings round about.

In such cases the *-ing* part of the verb has almost the force of a predicative adjective.

5 Both the simple and the progressive forms of the present tense may be used with a future reference if the verb is in the active voice.

We leave for the Continent on Friday.
We are leaving for the Continent on Friday.

The simple form represents the fact as something that is fixed and is unlikely to be altered. It is rather impersonal. The progressive form represents it as the present arrangement in respect of the future, and implies a more personal interest. Often there is a suggestion of intention attached to it. Thus if we wished to drop a hint to someone who had not been to see us for some time that a visit would be appreciated, we should ask,

When are you coming to see us?
not, When do you come to see us?

If the reference is to a special or exceptional arrangement, applying to one specific occasion, the progressive form is generally used. Thus *I finish work early tomorrow* implies that that is the usual practice on that particular day of the week. But *I am finishing work early tomorrow* implies that it is an exception to the usual rule.

6 In the passive voice, when the reference is to the future, the progressive form of the present tense is normal, but not the simple form.

The matter *is being discussed* at the next meeting of the committee. (not *the matter is discussed*)
The matter is to be discussed ......

EXERCISES

1 Fill in the blanks in the following sentences with the simple or the progressive form (present tense) of the verb given in brackets at the end of each.

a The Italians ..... in Italy. (live)
b Mr Johnson ..... to the office in his car each morning. (go)
c My aunt ..... with us for a few weeks. (stay)
d Jack cannot come out to play just now, as he ..... his homework. (do)
e We ..... to the seaside for a month every summer. (go)
f A vegetarian is a person who never ..... meat. (eat)
g An honest person always ..... the truth. (tell)
h The workmen ..... the road near our house. (repair)
i My husband will see you in about quarter of an hour; he ..... his lunch at the moment. (have)
j There are some birds that ..... every year. (migrate)
k A person who ..... ladies' hats is known as a milliner. (sell)
l That child ..... because it cannot find its mother. (cry)

m My sister and I ..... to the cinema every Thursday evening. (go)
n The Pyrenees ..... France from Spain. (divide)
o It was very dull early this morning, but the sun ..... now. (shine)

2 Complete the following sentences by supplying the correct form of the verb given at the end of each. Use the present tense.

a ..... you ..... playing football? (like)
b A teetotaller ..... not ..... wine. (drink)
c ..... the doctor ..... to see your brother every day? (call)
d ..... you ..... tea or coffee? (prefer)
e ..... your uncle ..... that house? (own)
f ..... the workmen still ..... your house? (repair)
g ..... you ..... to read mystery stories? (like)
h ..... the floods still .....? (rise)
i ..... anyone ..... where Susan has gone? (know)
j How often .....you.....to the cinema? (go)
k Why ..... that child .....? (cry)
l ..... you ..... or .....you ..... it seriously? (joke, mean)
m ..... the cinemas ..... on Sunday in your town? (open)
n Where ..... your friend .... when he goes to London? (stay)
o To which station ..... I ..... to get a train for Liverpool? (go)

3 For each of the following verbs compose one sentence of your own containing the simple form of the present tense, and one containing the progressive form:

eat, write, live, learn, sit, sleep, read, walk, stand, fly

4 Write five sentences containing the progressive form of the present tense used with a future reference. Each sentence should contain a different verb.

B. SIMPLE AND PROGRESSIVE FORMS OF THE PAST TENSE

1 The difference between the two forms of the past tense is basically the same as that between the corresponding forms of the present.

(*a*) The progressive form represents an activity as being in progress at some point of time in the past.

When we arrived they *were having* lunch.

(*b*) The simple form represents something that was recurrent, habitual, or general.

We *had* lunch at 12.30 in those days.
In the Middle Ages people *believed* that the earth was flat.

2 But there are two other uses of the simple form of the past that for most verbs have no parallel in the present.

(*a*) It may represent an activity or occurrence on one particular occasion, but viewed retrospectively.

We had lunch at one o'clock today.
As he entered the room he took off his hat.
The train arrived ten minutes late.

(*b*) It may represent an activity which, though progressive in nature, is viewed in its entirety, after its completion.

He waded into the middle of the pond to retrieve his hat.
She climbed the stairs very slowly.
I slept for three hours.

3 Sometimes it makes very little difference to the meaning whether we use the simple or the progressive form. This applies mainly to verbs of the following two kinds.

(*a*) Where the activity is a momentary one, so that the difference between progress and completion is scarcely distinguishable.

The intruder was caught as he left (was leaving) the premises.
A shot was fired at the train as it entered (was entering) the tunnel.

(*b*) Where the completed activity is a continuance of the same state, process or situation; or where the situation is such that we cannot think of any kind of completion.

A vase of flowers stood (was standing) in the centre of the table.
Two men sat (were sitting) at the table on our left.

Generally the progressive form is more vivid and descriptive than the simple form. The former presents the situation from the point of view of the speaker, as he appreciated it at the moment. The latter is rather more impersonal and detached.

EXERCISES

Fill in the blank spaces in the following sentences with either the simple or the progressive form of the past tense of the verb given at the end of each (whichever you think is appropriate).

1. He ..... the room and ..... down in the chair. (cross, sit)
2. When we set out early this morning the sun ..... (shine)
3. As he ..... the road a bus.....him down. (cross, knock)
4. The passenger in the next seat to me ..... a newspaper. (read)
5. He ..... and ...... his leg as he was alighting from a bus. (slip, injure)
6. My grandfather was seventy-five years old when he ..... (die)
7. When the doctor arrived he realised that the patient ..... (die)
8. The sound of their conversation .... the baby. (waken)
9. We were told that the manager could not see us at that moment, as he ..... some letters to his secretary. (dictate)
10. When he took off his hat I noticed that his hair ..... grey. (go)
11. My husband ..... quite a lot of money for that picture. (pay)
12. At one time it ..... several weeks to get from Britain to America by sea. (take)
13. A schoolboy ..... a purse full of money lying in the gutter. (find)
14. We ..... someone opening the gate. (hear)
15. When we ..... he ..... the lawn. (arrive, mow)

C. THE PERFECT TENSE

The perfect tense (made up from the past participle of a verb preceded by the present tense of the auxiliary *have*: *I have eaten, they have gone*) is the tense that is used when we wish to express the idea that some activity that took place in the past, or a situation that originated in the past, is connected in some way with the present. It may be the recent past that is referred to (*I have just finished my dinner*), a more distant past, or an indeterminate past (*I have lived in the East*). The nearness or remoteness of the time is not material, for the perfect tense merely states the position at the present moment.

We may distinguish four main uses of it, as follows:

1 *The Continuative Use* This states something that has been continuous from the past up to the present moment.

> We have known each other for the past ten years.
> We have lived in this house since 1952. (or *have been living*)
> I have never drunk alcoholic liquor.

Here the implication is that the situation still exists: we still know each other; we still live in this house; I still do not drink alcoholic liquor.

2 *The Inclusive Use* This represents a completed activity or occurrence falling *within* a period extending from some point of time in the past up to the present.

> There have been two major wars during the present century.
> My father has seen the Niagara Falls.
> He has been a teacher, a sales representative, a bookseller, and now he is a journalist.

This use of the perfect is often employed when we are speaking or writing about the career of a person who is still living.

> He has held the following offices.

It also occurs with *before*, when *before* means ' some time in the past, reckoning back from the present moment '.

> I have seen that fellow somewhere before.

3 *The Resultative Use* This represents an activity completed in the past—either recent or more remote, as:

(*a*) Giving rise to a certain result in the present:

I have had my lunch. (Implication: so I do not need it now)
You have told us that already. (Implication: so you do not need to tell us again)
We have bought a television set. (Result: so we now have a television set)
You have torn your coat. (Result: there is a tear in your coat)

(*b*) Deducible from resulting signs or evidence:

Someone has dropped some crockery. (Evidence: I have just heard the crash)
It has rained during the night. (Evidence: the ground is wet.)
Someone has called while we have been out. (Evidence: the gate is open.)

In (*a*) the emphasis is usually on the resultant position, in (*b*) on the inference from the result.

4 *The Perfect of Experience* This states what has occurred, or what has been the case, within the speaker's or the writer's experience.

I have known it snow in May.
I have seen many a promising career ruined by drink.

The important thing to remember about all four of these uses is that the perfect tense must not be accompanied by an adverb or adverbial expression denoting past time.. If the activity or the fact is assigned to a definite time in the past, and so cut off from the present, then the simple form of the past tense must be used.

I *saw* that film last week. (not I *have seen* that film last week.)

The following two tables set out examples of the right and the wrong use of the perfect tense, with instructions for correcting the wrong uses.

Correct Uses of the Perfect
I have had my dinner.
We have had a very enjoyable holiday.
I have had my bicycle repaired.
She has slept for eight hours.

Incorrect Use	*Correction*
I have had my dinner an hour ago.	I had my dinner an hour ago.
We have had a very enjoyable holiday last summer.	We had a very enjoyable holiday last summer.
I have had my bicycle repaired yesterday.	I had my bicycle repaired yesterday.
She has slept for eight hours last night.	She slept for eight hours last night.

Ask yourself why those in the first column are wrong, and why the correction shown in the second column is necessary.

Words and expressions like *this morning* and *this afternoon*, which denote a particular part of the day, may take either the perfect or the past tense, according to circumstances. For instance, if it is still morning when we are speaking we should probably say:

> I *have had* so many interruptions this morning that I *have done* scarcely any work.

But if we are speaking later in the same day (about 3 p.m.), when the morning is a past period of time, we should say:

> I *had* so many interruptions this morning that I *did* scarcely any work.

Even if it is still morning, however, it does not necessarily follow that we should use the perfect; it depends on whether we feel that the fact we are relating has, or has not, some connexion with the moment of speaking. Thus if we were speaking immediately on our arrival at work, when the annoyance caused by traffic delays was fresh in our mind, we should probably say:

I can usually get here in about thirty-five minutes, but it *has taken* me nearly an hour this morning.

But later in the morning, when we are looking back at it and it has become something that belongs to the past, we should say:

It *took* me nearly an hour to get here this morning.

For similar reasons we might say either:

I *saw* your friend Peter today.

or

I *have seen* your friend Peter today.

In the former case the speaker thinks of the meeting as an isolated occurrence that took place several hours ago, and therefore belongs to the past. In the latter case he thinks of it as something that is included in, and forms part of, all that he has done and that has happened to him in a day that is not yet ended.

Finally there is the case of the two sentences,

I *have come* to ask your advice. (Perfect)

and

I *came* to ask your advice. (Past)

The former would be used by a person immediately on his arrival, to announce the purpose of his visit. It might also be used some time after his arrival, when, following some preliminary conversation, he finally gets round to the real object of his visit. In that case he links his purpose with his presence in the room at that moment. But in such a situation he might also say,

I came to ask your advice.

In that case he would be linking his purpose with his arrival some while previously, i.e., with some event in the past.

Even when he is making the announcement immediately on his arrival, if it was obvious to him that the purpose with which he had come was not to be fulfilled, he would probably use *came* rather than *have come*, referring to the purpose he had in view on setting out instead of presenting it as one he has at the moment of speaking.

I came to see Mr Smith, but I understand that he is not here today.

N.B. In more formal English the simple form of the present tense is sometimes used instead of the perfect, when the verb is followed by some expression denoting purpose.

I come to ask your advice.
'I come to bury Cæsar, not to praise him.'
Mr Chairman, I rise on a point of order.

In spoken English, the present tense *hear*, followed by a clause stating the nature of the news, is generally used instead of *have heard* when the speaker implies that he accepts the news as probably true.

I hear that you have got a new car.

It is, however, confined to positive statements. In negative statements and in questions the perfect is used.

Have you heard that Sheila is engaged to be married?
We know that he sat for the examination, but we have not heard that he passed.

(*We have not heard whether he passed* expresses no opinion on the matter, but *We have not heard that he passed* implies that, in the absence of any information, we assume that he probably did not.)

EXERCISES

1 Insert in the blank spaces in the sentences below the past or the perfect tense (whichever you think is correct) of the verb given at the end.

a We ..... to the theatre last evening. (go)
b My father ..... sixty years old last Tuesday. (be)
c Do you know whether the doctor ..... yet? (be)
d ..... you ..... the film that is showing at the Odeon? (see)
e We ..... to this house in 1935 and ..... here ever since. (come, live)
f It ..... every day this week. (rain)
g No-one ..... from him for the past six months. (hear)
h Last Saturday we ..... to visit some friends in a neighbouring town. (go)

i We ..... all our money, so we shall have to walk home. (spend)
j Shakespeare ..... from 1564 to 1616. (live)
k ..... the postman ..... yet? (come)
l We ..... you already that we cannot do what you ask. (tell)
m When I ..... a boy we ..... on a farm. (*be, live*)
n The weather ..... warmer yesterday than it is today. (be)
o Mrs Smith is not at home; she ..... to visit some friends. (go)
p She ..... out at ten o'clock, and ..... not yet ..... (go, return)
q Several books on that subject ..... during the present year. (appear)
r I cannot play in the match as I ..... my foot. (injure)
s I ..... to him last week, but he ..... not ..... yet. (write, reply)
t The accident ..... at 10.30 this morning. (occur)

2 Compose two sentences for each of the following verbs. In the first sentence of each pair use the past tense, and in the second use the perfect.

buy; find; open; call; learn; read; write; walk; stop; fall; finish; drink; help; break; invent

3 Compose ten sentences of your own, and in each of the sentences include one of the following words or expressions. In each case use the past or the perfect tense of the verb (whichever you think is correct).

(*a*) yesterday, (*b*) this year, (*c*) since last August, (*d*) this afternoon, (*e*) for the last three months, (*f*) last week, (*g*) in 1945, (*h*) since her illness, (*i*) on his twenty-first birthday, (*j*) every day this week.

D. THE PROGRESSIVE FORM OF THE PERFECT

As the progressive (or continuous) form of the present is made from the present participle preceded by the present tense of the auxiliary *be*, (*I am studying English*), so the progressive (or continuous) form of the perfect is made from the present participle preceded by the perfect form of the auxiliary (*I have been studying English for three years*).

The progressive form of the present represents only what is in progress at the moment of speaking (*I am writing a letter. The door-bell is ringing*). If we wish to indicate that the action or occurrence has been going on continuously or repeatedly over a period of time starting in the past and extending right up to the present, then we must use the progressive form of the perfect.

> I *have been writing* letters since ten o'clock this morning.
> (not *I am writing letters since ten o'clock this morning.*)
> The door-bell *has been ringing* for the past ten minutes.
> (not *The door-bell is ringing for the past ten minutes.*)

This is the progressive counterpart of the continuative use of the perfect, described on p. 87.

Another use is to represent as in some way connected with the present, the progressive performance in the past of some activity which is now complete, i.e., which does not itself extend up to the present, but is for some reason felt to fall within the present time-sphere.

> I have been washing my car.
> We have been looking at the pictures.

This is the progressive counterpart of the resultative and the inclusive uses of the perfect, mentioned on p. 87. *I have washed my car* merely states the final result; *I have been washing my car* introduces us to the whole process as it was carried out from start to finish.

There is no progressive counterpart of the perfect of experience, for the simple reason that things that form part of our experience are things that we view retrospectively, in their completed state.

The progressive form is essentially a form denoting *duration*; and just as the ordinary form of the perfect cannot be accompanied by any adverbial expression denoting a point of time in the past, so the progressive form of the perfect cannot be accompanied by any adverbial expression denoting duration of time in the past and unconnected with the present.

EXERCISES

Insert the correct form of the auxiliary in the following sentences in order to complete the sense.

1. It has been fine most of the morning, but it ..... raining now.
2. It ..... raining since ten o'clock.
3. I ..... waiting here for almost half an hour.
4. The doctor ..... visiting his patients all the morning.
5. The Joneses ..... coming to dinner this evening.
6. My son ..... going to that school for the past five years.
7. When I first knew him he ..... living in Birmingham.
8. The sick man ..... improving steadily all the week.
9. The thieves ran away when they learned that the police..... coming.
10. The baby ..... sleeping ever since six o'clock.

E. TENSES WITH *SINCE*

Since, when used to denote time, means ' from some specified point of time in the past up to and including the present moment '. Because it thus connects a past activity or situation with the present, it follows that:

(*a*) It must normally be preceded by the *perfect* tense of the verb.

> I *have not seen* him since last January. (not *did not see* or *do not see*)
> We *have lived* here since the year 1948. (not *We live here*)

(*b*) When we wish to say that an activity or a process has been going on continuously since the time specified, and is still going on, we must use the progressive form of the perfect.

> It *has been raining* since eight o'clock this morning. (not *It is raining*)

(*c*) If the past point of time from which we reckon is indicated by an adverb clause of time introduced by *since*, then the verb of this clause must be in the *past* tense.

> I have not seen him since we *left* school. (not *have left*)
> We have lived in this house ever since my father *died*. (not *has died*)
> Since he *changed* his job he has been much happier. (not *has changed*)

The general rule is, then, that the verb of the main clause is in the perfect tense, and that *since* is followed either by a word or phrase denoting past time (*since the war*, *since* 1955, *since last week*), or by a clause in which the verb is in the past tense. But there are exceptions to this. They are as follows:

(*a*) When the main clause is a statement or a question concerning the length of time between the point of reckoning in the past and the moment of speaking (i.e., the present 'sum' of it) the present, not the perfect tense, is used in this clause.

> It *is* fourteen years since I saw him. (not *has been*)
> It seems a long time since our last holiday. (not *has seemed*)
> How long *is* it since you had a rise in salary? (not *has it been?*)

(*b*) When the point from which we reckon in the past is the beginning of a situation which has persisted throughout and still exists, then the perfect tense is used in the 'since' clause instead of the past.

> He has never been to visit me since I *have been* ill.
> He has borne a good character ever since I *have known* him.

Since I have been ill implies that I am still ill; *since I was ill* would imply that I am no longer ill, i.e., that he came to visit me during my illness, but as soon as I recovered his visits ceased. And similar considerations would apply to the other example.

EXERCISES

1 Fill in the blank spaces in the following sentences with the correct tense of the verb given in brackets at the end.

a We ..... nothing to eat since eight o'clock this morning. (have)
b That child ..... very much since I last ..... her. (grow, saw)
c It ..... almost five years since my brother left for America. (be)
d Her health ..... greatly since she ..... to live in the country. (improve, go)
e He ..... not ..... to us since last Christmas. (write)

f Ever since he .... that accident he ..... with a limp. (have, walk)
g I ..... more highly of him as a writer since I ..... his last novel. (think, read)
h Since my son ..... to that school he ..... rapid progress. (go, make)
i They ..... not ..... to each other since they had that quarrel. (speak)
j It ..... continuously since six o'clock this morning. (rain)
k He ..... three jobs since he ..... work five years ago. (have, start)
l Since her husband ..... she ..... very unhappy. (die, be)

2 Complete the following sentences by adding words of your own.

a I have known him since ..... (use a clause)
b ...... since we had our holiday.
c ..... since the end of the war.
d I have not seen a good film since .....
e Since I learned to drive a car .....
f ..... since he had that illness.
g No less than five different people have lived in that house since ..... (use a clause)
h No-one has heard from him since .....
i ..... since the Joneses went to London.
j Since ..... I have felt very much better.

F. TENSES IN ADVERB CLAUSES REFERRING TO THE FUTURE

In a main clause indicating future time, the future tense or its equivalent is used,[1] but in an adverb clause dependent on it the present tense is the normal one—usually the simple form.

> I *shall call* and see you when I *come* to London. (not *when I shall come*)
> We *go* away for our holiday as soon as the children *finish* school. (not *will finish*)
> I *intend calling* to see you when next I *come* to London.

[1] See p. 171

The following table gives a number of examples with different kinds of subordinating conjunctions as introductory words. Not all the adverb clauses are clauses of time, but all refer to the future.

I shall not come	unless I hear from you.
You will fail	unless you work harder.
We shall not go out	if it rains.[1]
I shall take my umbrella	in case it rains.[1]
We shall start	as soon as we are ready.
My son will be twenty	when I am forty-eight.
I am going to buy a new car	when the price comes down.

In most of the above sentences the order of the clauses could be reversed, the adverb clause being put first; but this makes no difference to the tenses.

Notes

1. Remember that when such sentences as the above are put into reported (i.e. indirect) speech, the *shall* or *will* of the main clause is converted to *should* or *would*, and the present tense of the subordinate clause is changed to the corresponding past tense. Just as *shall* and *will* do not normally appear in the subordinate clause of the direct form, so *should* and *would* must not normally appear in the subordinate clause of the indirect.

> He said *he would not come* unless he *heard* from me.
> He said that no-one *would leave* before the bell *went*.
> I told them that I *should take* my umbrella in case it *rained*.

2. The auxiliary *will* may occur in the subordinate clause, but only in such sentences as:

> I will do it if you *will help* me.

Here *will* expresses, not a future, but a present, meaning 'if you are willing'.

3. Such sentences as the following, in which a future is used, are correct:

[1] *If it should rain* and *in case it should rain* are also possible; but these express a contingency which is thought rather unlikely.

Call again this afternoon, when *I shall have* more time to see you.
Go to the main entrance, where *you will find* a messenger waiting.

But in this case the second clause is not really a subordinate one; it is co-ordinate with the first. *When* means ' for then ', or ' and then '. *Where* means ' and there '.

4. In certain cases the progressive form of the present tense is possible in the adverb clause, if the situation or the activity is thought of as being in progress at the time referred to.

We shall not go out	if it is raining.
We shall not come in	if you are watching the television.
Do not come to work tomorrow	if you are not feeling better.
Give me a ring[1]	if you are expecting visitors.

EXERCISES

Insert in the blank spaces in the following sentences the correct tense of the verb given in brackets at the end.

a You will not succeed unless you ..... harder. (work)
b I will let you know as soon as I ..... any information. (have)
c Do not do anything further until you ..... from me. (hear)
d We shall go for a walk when it ..... raining. (stop)
e We must have everything ready before the guests ..... (arrive)
f We cannot come to a decision before we ..... the facts. (know)
g We should like to reach home before it ..... dark. (get)
h Nothing can be done until we ..... his answer. (receive)
i She will inherit a fortune of £20,000 when she ..... the age of twenty-one. (attain)
j We had better take some food with us, in case the shops ..... closed. (be)
k When I ..... enough money, I intend to buy a car. (have)
l There will be a rush for seats when the train ..... (arrive)

[1] A colloquialism meaning ' Telephone me '.

m You will think very differently from this when you ..... older. (be)
n Think carefully before you ..... (answer)
o When George ..... twenty, John will be twenty-three. (be)

G. TENSES IN ADJECTIVE CLAUSES REFERRING TO THE FUTURE

An adjective clause referring to the future may take either (*a*) a future tense, or (*b*) a present tense. Which of the two we use depends on the way we regard the fact that it expresses. If we think of it in relation to the moment at which we are speaking (i.e. the present moment), then we see it as a future event or situation, and we use the future tense. But if we think of it in relation to another future event or situation (usually the one in which its antecedent is involved) with which it is more or less co-temporaneous, then the present tense is used. Here are some sentences which will illustrate the point.

> You are to bring me the papers which you *will find* on my desk.

Here the idea of finding the papers is thought of in relation to the moment when the speaker is giving the instruction; it is therefore represented as a future event, and the future tense is used. The same is true also of the following.

> You must show no-one the note which the attendant *will give* you.
> I intend to pay for my new house with the money I *shall get* from the sale of this one.

But now contrast these with the following:

> I shall get on the first bus that *comes*.

Here the speaker is projecting his mind into the future and thinking of the bus coming while he is waiting, so he uses the present tense. Similarly we have:

> We shall award the prize to the person who *gets* the highest marks.
> I shall pay the bill with the money he *gives* me.

We cannot consider applications that *are received* after June 30th.

This cup will be presented to the competitor who *wins* the race.

The present tense is also used if the reference is to a fact or situation which, though viewed in a future setting, does not apply exclusively to the future.

When I retire I shall go to live in a place where the climate *is* warmer than it is here.

She has promised that she will never marry a person who *drinks*.

The present tense is much more frequent than the future. The latter often suggests that it is already known that the event in question will occur. *You must show no-one the note which the attendant will give you* implies that the speaker already knows that the person to whom the instruction is addressed will be given a note by the attendant. And similarly *You are to bring me the papers which you will find on my desk* implies that the speaker knows (or at least assumes) that the papers will be found there. This, however, does not preclude his using the present tense, and so presenting the fact as though he did not know. If the context makes it clear that he does not know, then the future tense cannot be used.

We shall not wait for anyone who arrives late.

EXERCISES

Insert in the blank spaces in the following sentences the correct tense of the verb given in brackets at the end.

1. I shall buy the hat that ..... cheapest. (be)
2. We shall appoint the person who ..... the best qualifications for the post. (have)
3. As soon as he ....., show him to my office. (arrive)
4. You are to go in by the main entrance, which you ..... on your right . (find)
5. You should report at once any suspicious circumstances you ..... (notice)
6. Anyone who ..... late will not be admitted. (come)

7. Make sure you take with you all the tools you ..... for the job. (need)
8. Is there a train that ..... me to London about midday? (get)
9. We intend to have lunch at the first restaurant we ..... (see)
10. The first person who ..... the correct answer will be awarded the prize. (get)
11. You are not to admit anyone who ..... a ticket. (have, use the negative)
12. I want a brief case that ..... me until I retire from business. (last)

H. TENSES IN CONDITIONAL SENTENCES

There are three kinds of condition:

1 Open Condition, i.e., a condition which may or may not be fulfilled.

> If it rains, the match will be cancelled. (It may rain, or it may not; we do not know.)

For this, if the reference is to the present, we use the present tense in both the conditional and the main clause.

> If I *eat* cheese, it *gives* me indigestion.
> If water *freezes*, it *turns* to ice.
> If it *is* only ten o'clock, we still *have* time to catch the train.

If the reference is to the future, the present tense is used in the conditional clause, and the future tense in the main clause.

> If I *have* time, *I shall visit* the exhibition.
> If I *see* a suitable present for her, I *shall buy* it.

N.B. When the main clause gives an order or an instruction, the future tense is, of course, replaced by the imperative.

> If you *get* a chance to speak to him, *ask* him how his family are getting on.

In sentences referring to the past, two patterns are possible.

(*a*) If the reference is to something that is general or habitual, then usually the past tense is used in both clauses.

> If there *was* a rush of orders, we *had* to work overtime.
> If the manager *received* any complaints, he *investigated* them personally.

(*b*) If the reference is to a specific occurrence or situation which, though it may belong to the past now, was future when regarded from a particular point of time in the past, then the past tense is used in the conditional clause, and the future in the past (or conditional) tense in the other clause.

> We decided that, if it *was* fine, we *would walk* home.
> I *hoped* that, if I *rested* for a few days, I *should feel* much better.

N.B. *would* (for all persons) is sometimes used also in sentences expressing repetition or a general practice.

> If he had a few hours to spare, he *would spend* them in the library.

This is the counterpart of a similar use of *will* in the present.

> He *will* sometimes sit for hours reading a book.

2 Rejected Condition, i.e., a condition which might have been fulfilled, but is not. For this we use the past subjunctive in the conditional clause if the verb is *to be*, and the past indicative if it is any other verb. The main clause has the future in the past (or conditional) tense.

> We *could* start dinner if only John *were* here.
> If I *weren't* so tired, I *would go* for a walk with you.
> If I *had* time, I *should visit* the exhibition.

(These sentences imply that John is not here, that I am tired, and that I have not time.)

If the reference is to the past, this becomes:

> We *could have started* dinner if only John *had been* there.
> If I *had not been* so tired, I *would have gone* for a walk with you.
> If I *had had* time, I *should have visited* the exhibition.
> If he *had studied* harder, he *would have passed* the examination.

3 Imaginary Condition, i.e., one which could not be true (*If I were you*), or which, even if it is not impossible, is not seriously contemplated, but is only advanced for the sake of argument.

> If I were a millionaire .....
> If you were attacked by a bandit .....

Here, again, we generally use the past subjunctive, in the conditional clause if the verb is *to be*, and the past indicative of other verbs, while the main clause has the future in the past (conditional).[1]

> If I *were* a millionaire I *would give* generously to good causes.
> What *would* you *do* if you *were attacked* by a bandit?
> If he *had* all the wealth in the world he *would not be* happy.

If the reference is to past time, *were* becomes *had been*, and *would/should* becomes *would have/should have*.

> What *would* you *have done* if you *had been attacked* by a bandit?
> I *should not have tolerated* his rudeness, if I *had been* you.

EXERCISES

1 Complete the following sentences by inserting in the blank spaces the correct part of any verb you think suitable in order to make a clause of *open* condition.

a If it ..... we shall not go out.
b If you ..... ill you should see a doctor.
c We will have a game of tennis tomorrow, if the weather ..... suitable.
d If you ..... a mistake, you should correct it.
e Mr Brown always cycled to work if the weather ..... fine.

---

[1] In colloquial English, even with *to be*, the past indicative (*was*) is often used with a singular subject for both rejected and imaginary condition.

> If your father *was* here, he would be disgusted at your conduct.
> If I *was* a millionaire, I should give generously to good causes.

But we always say *If I were you* (not *If I was you*), probably because, on account of frequent repetition, it has become a set expression, and so the subjunctive is perpetuated.

f I shall leave the office at 4.30 if nothing ..... me.
g If the train ..... punctually, we shall be in London just before three o'clock.
h If an accident ..... you should report it at once to the police.
i I shall call and see him tomorrow evening if I ..... time.
j When I was a schoolboy we were punished if we ..... late more than once in the same week.

2 Complete the following sentences by inserting in the blank spaces the correct part of any verb you think suitable in order to make a clause of *rejected* or *imaginary* condition.

a If I ..... you I should refuse to accept his excuse.
b If only we ..... two minutes earlier, we should have caught the train.
c If you ..... me, I could have helped you.
d If he ..... more careful, the accident would not have happened.
e If I ..... his address, I would have called on him.
f I could never have solved the problem if you ..... me. (Use a negative verb.)
g If they ..... my advice, they would not have made this mistake.
h If I ..... old enough, I would join the Air Force.
i Nothing could have saved your life if you ..... over that cliff.

3 Add a main clause to the following conditional clauses in order to complete the sentence.

a If it is not too far
b If he had learned his lesson properly
c If I have enough money
d If I had known they were here
e If I can get away from the office in time
f If everyone were to do just what he liked
g If you had carried out the instructions
h If you need any assistance
i If you would like a ticket for the concert
j If I were a Member of Parliament

4 Put the following conditional sentences into the past.

a If it is fine, we always walk to work.
b If I were you, I should not accept the post.
c If she has any free time, she spends it in the garden.
d If I sold this house, I should get at least £ 4,000 for it.
e If she needs any advice, she always comes to me for it.
f If I tell the truth, no-one will believe me.
g If you spoke more slowly, we should hear you better.
h We could buy a new car if only we had a little more money.
i What would you do if you missed the last train?
j If he were a year older, he would be eligible for the post.

17. Redundant pronouns and prepositions in complex sentences

1 *Pronouns*

When two simple sentences are combined to make a complex sentence, a noun or pronoun in one of them will be replaced by the relative pronoun *which*, *that*, *who*, *whom*, or *whose*. The noun or pronoun thus replaced must not be used as well as the relative. Take the following example.

I have found the book. I lost *it* yesterday.

When these are combined, *it* becomes *which* or *that*, and so disappears from the sentence.

I have found the book which I lost yesterday.
or I have found the book that I lost yesterday.
But not
I have found the book which I lost *it* yesterday.
or ..... that I lost *it* yesterday.

2 *Prepositions*

When the noun or pronoun which is converted to the relative is preceded by a preposition, the preposition remains, and is usually placed before the relative.

This is the person. I gave the money *to him.*

These two sentences combined become:

This is the person *to whom* I gave the money.

It is often possible, however, to place the preposition at the end of the sentence:

This is the person *whom* I gave the money *to.*

It is *always* placed at the end:

(*a*) When the relative pronoun is *that.*

This is the car that we came *in.* (not *in that we came*)

(*b*) When the relative pronoun is omitted altogether.

There is the person we were looking *for.*

But the preposition must never be placed before the relative, and at the end of the sentence as well. We must not say:

Here is the information *for* which you asked *for.*

The two correct alternatives are:

Here is the information for which you asked.
Here is the information (which) you asked for.

EXERCISES

Combine the following pairs of simple sentences to make a complex sentence, by converting one of each pair to a relative (adjectival) clause.

A
1. This is the watch. I had it for my birthday .
2. That is the house. I mentioned it to you just now.
3. I am going to read that book. You recommended it to me.
4. Do you remember that strange person? We met him in the café.
5. I gave the porter a tip. He thanked me for it.
6. We saw a film. It was very interesting.
7. He will give you a message. You must remember it.
8. She wore a dress. It was made of silk.
9. We have eaten all the food. We brought it with us.
10. I overheard the story. My neighbour was telling it to his friend.

B 1. That is the field. We used to play in it.
2. Here is the magazine. You were looking for it.
3. He pointed out the car. The visitors came in it.
4. The police examined the safe. The money had been stolen from it.
5. We gazed at the object. The guide was pointing to it.
6. That is the weapon. The murder was committed with it.
7. She showed me the envelope. The letter was enclosed in it.
8. We went to the spot. They directed us to it.
9. This is the seat. I was sitting in it.
10. The man sitting opposite to me offered to lend me the newspaper. He had been looking at it.

18. Redundant conjunctions in complex sentences

In English, when two sentences are combined so that they make one sentence, only *one* conjunction, or other joining word, is used to connect them. Take for example the following.

She was tired. She still went on working.

These two sentences may be combined in either of the following two ways:

(*a*) By using a co-ordinating conjunction, which places both the clauses, grammatically, on an equal footing.

She was tired, *but* she still went on working.

(*b*) By using a subordinating conjunction, and thus converting one of the sentences to a subordinate clause.

Although she was tired, she still went on working.

The following, however, where both conjunctions are used, is not correct.

Although she was tired, *but* she still sent on working.

He transgressed the law. He was punished.

These may be combined in either of the following ways:

(*a*) He transgressed the law, *so* he was punished.
(*b*) *Because* he transgressed the law, he was punished.

But not, *Because* he transgressed the law, *so* he was punished.

EXERCISES

Combine the following pairs of sentences in two ways, so as to make one sentence consisting of two clauses.

1. We missed the last bus. We had to walk home.
2. The task was very difficult. We managed to complete it.
3. It was a fine day. They decided to go for a walk.
4. The train was late in arriving. I missed my appointment.
5. I warned him of the danger. He took no notice.
6. He had finished his work. He left the office early.
7. The ground was unfit to play on. The match had to be abandoned.
8. No public transport was running. The employees were on strike.
9. He tried repeatedly. He could not succeed.
10. She promised to come early. She has not arrived yet.

19. Introductory *there*

1 In a statement the subject normally precedes the verb.

A page is missing from this book.

If the sentence is so framed that the subject follows the verb instead of preceding it (or, in the case of a compound tense, if the subject follows the auxiliary), then its place before the verb must be supplied by the introductory word *there*. This cannot be omitted.

There is a page missing from this book. (not *Is a page missing from this book.*)
There was a dreadful thunderstorm last night. (not *Was a dreadful thunderstorm last night.*)
There once lived a very rich king. (not *Once lived a very rich king.*)
There has been a railway accident. (not *Has been a railway accident.*)

2 In interrogative sentences *there* follows the verb (or in the case of compound tenses follows the auxiliary), just as a subject would do in such sentences.

Is there a page missing from your book?
Was there a thunderstorm last night?
Has there been an accident?

3 The verb is always third person, but in number it agrees with the ' real ' subject that follows it.

There *is* a horse in the stable.
There *are* three cows in the field.
Was there a good attendance at the meeting?
Were there many guests at the wedding?

In this connexion the following points should be noticed.

(*a*) *A lot of* and *plenty of* take a plural verb when they denote number, and a singular verb when they denote quantity or amount.

There *were* a lot of people at the exhibition.
There *are* a lot of streams in this district.
There *are* plenty of opportunities for well-qualified people.
There *is* a lot of water in the well.
There *is* plenty of time.

A number of always takes a plural verb, since it means *several*, or *many*.

There *have* been a number of accidents at that spot.

(*b*) A singular collective noun, like *a crowd of people*, *a gang of thieves*, *a company of soldiers*, *a group of boys*, takes a singular verb.

There *was* a crowd of people at the street corner.

(*c*) *A dozen,* since it denotes a plural number, takes a plural verb.

There *are* a dozen eggs in that basket.

But *a pair,* when applied to things like scissors, shoes, trousers, where the two components are always thought of together, takes a singular verb.

There *was* a pair of trousers in the wardrobe.
Is there a pair of shoes in that cupboard?

4 *There is/are* is also used to denote the mere existence of something. The word *there* must not be omitted.

There is a saying that the third time is lucky. (not *Is a saying*)
At one time there were houses where that large factory now stands. (not *At one time were houses*)

Often also it denotes an occurrence.

There was a loud explosion. (i.e., a loud explosion occurred)
There is to be an inquiry into the cause of the accident. (i.e., an inquiry is to take place)

Again care must be taken not to omit the introductory *there,* for without it the sentence would be incorrect.

EXERCISES

1 Rewrite the following sentences so as to bring out the same meaning by using the introductory word *there.*

a Two people were sitting at the next table to ours.
b A policeman was standing at the entrance to the hall.
c Something is wrong with this clock.
d A time will come when you will regret your folly.
e A seat happened to be vacant in the back row.
f Sentries were posted all round the building.
g Three cars were involved in the accident.
h Nothing was to be seen but vast stretches of grassland.
i A time comes in everyone's life when he has to give up work.
j Over a hundred people were present at the lecture.

2 Give answers to the following questions, using the introductory word *there.*

a How many days are there in a week?
b Is there a library in this town?
c Are there any tickets left for tonight's concert?
d Is there a post office near here?
e What time is there a train to London?
f Is there a dining car on that train?
g Was anyone injured when the cars collided?
h Could you please tell me where there is a chemist's shop?
i How many books are there on that shelf?
j How many pupils are there in your class?

3 Insert *was* or *were* (whichever you think correct) in the blank space in the following sentences.

a We shouted several times, but there ..... no answer.
b There ..... nothing we could do to help the injured man.
c There ..... papers scattered all over the floor.
d Suddenly there ..... a loud explosion.
e There ..... no room for any more passengers on the bus.
f When we arrived there ..... already a number of people there.
g There ..... plenty of food for everyone.
h There ..... no-one who could tell us the way.
i There ..... a lot of houses damaged in that gale.
j As many of the guests who were expected did not turn up, there ..... a lot of food left.
k In that large garden there ..... plenty of room for the children to play.
l There ..... people of many nationalities staying at the hotel.
m .....there any chocolates left in that box?
n ..... there any reason for his late arrival?
o ..... there any letters for me by this morning's post?

20. The infinitive

A. WITH ANTICIPATORY *IT* AS SUBJECT

1 The infinitive, or the infinitive together with other words dependent on or subordinated to it, may sometimes be used as the subject of a finite verb.

To steal is wrong.
To play with explosives is dangerous.
To waste your money is foolish.

This construction, however, is rather formal; often, too, it is awkward, so instead we generally use an anticipatory *it* as the subject and then place the infinitive, in apposition to *it*, after the adjective. The following table gives the basic pattern.

It is wrong	to steal.
It is dangerous	to play with explosives.
It is foolish	to waste your money.
It is silly	to say that.
It is selfish	to take more than your fair share of food.
It is rude	to interrupt people's conversation.
It is impossible	to live without air.
It is difficult	to see in the dark.
It is not safe	to cross that bridge.

The same pattern may also occur with a noun instead of an adjective preceding the infinitive.

It is a shame	to cut down those trees.
It is a mistake	to put things off until the last minute.
It is a pity	to destroy those old houses.
It is a pleasure	to meet a cheerful person.
It was fun	to watch the antics of the monkeys.

All the statements in the first table are general ones, which are intended to apply to anyone. If we wish to restrict their application to specific people or groups of people[1], then we place a restrictive phrase beginning with *for* between the adjective and the infinitive. The noun or pronoun that follows *for* then becomes the subject of the infinitive. This is illustrated in the following table.

It is dangerous	for children	to play with fire.
It is easy	for a monkey	to climb trees.
It is rude	for the young	to make fun of their elders.
It is absurd	for you	to say that.
It is difficult	for a deaf person	to hear.
It is not safe	for lorries	to cross that bridge.
It was impossible	for us	to understand him.

This pattern is not so frequent after a noun (see table below) since usually the reference is already a specific one; but in a few cases a *for* adjunct is not impossible. When one is used, its effect is to direct the notion of the noun to the person performing the activity rather than to the activity itself.

It was a mistake	for us	to do that.
It is a shame	for you	to have to go to all that trouble.
It would be a pity	for us	to cancel the party.
It would be a pleasure	for me	to come with you.

2 There are some adjectives, mainly descriptive of moral or intellectual qualities, that can be applied both to a person and to something that he does. Thus we may speak of a *kind* person and a *kind* act, a *brave* person and a *brave* deed, a *foolish* person and a *foolish* action. Other adjectives that can be used in this way are *stupid*, *clever*, *right*, *wrong*, *good*, *wicked*, *courageous*, *cowardly*, *thoughtful*, *thoughtless*, *considerate*, *inconsiderate*, *cruel*, *generous*, *mean*, *careless*. These are only a few of the commoner ones. There are many others.

When we wish to apply such adjectives to a person in virtue of something that he does or has done, the preposition used is *of*. The pattern is as follows:

[1] It is usually people, but it may also be animals, or even non-animate things.

It is (was) + adjective/*of* + noun or pronoun denoting the person or persons/infinitive or infinitive construction denoting the action.

The table below will serve as an illustration.

It was very kind	of your uncle	to give us a lift in his car.
It was foolish	of you	to do that.
It is good	of your parents	to invite me.
It was brave	of him	to rescue that child.
It would be stupid	of us	to refuse the offer.
It was thoughtful	of John	to send me this present.
It was cruel	of those boys	to tease the cat.
It was wrong	of me	to put the blame on someone else.
It was quite right	of the teacher	to punish the pupil for dishonesty.

N.B. Adjectives such as *jealous*, *angry*, *cheerful*, *happy*, which can be applied only to persons, not to their actions, and those such as *possible*, *impossible*, *difficult*, *easy*, which refer to actions or situations, but not to persons, cannot be used in this pattern.

EXERCISES

1 Rewrite the following sentences, using the introductory word *it.*

a To take what belongs to another is wrong.
b To understand what he meant was difficult.
c To call people names is not polite.
d To sit by the fire on a cold evening is pleasant.
e To read your writing is impossible.
f To force the lock was necessary in order to open the door.
g To go by train would be best.
h To miss this opportunity would be a pity.
i To deceive your best friend is disgraceful.
j To entrust him with so large a sum of money was a mistake.

2 Expand the following into sentences by using the *for* adjunct as exemplified in the tables on p. 113 (Make different sentences from those given in the tables.)

a Is it safe .....?
b It is not easy .....
c It was impossible .....
d It is not fair .....
e It is dangerous .....
f I do not think it is right ......
g It is not good .....
h Is it necessary ..... ?
i Will it be possible .....?
j It is foolish.....

3 Copy out the first column of the table given on p. 114 (illustrating the use of the *of*-adjunct), and fill in the second and third columns with words of your own in order to make complete sentences.

4 Make up sentences on the same pattern as those in the table on p. 114, using the following adjectives:

greedy, cruel, clever, careless, mean, wise, thoughtful, cowardly, generous, silly.

Do not use the tabular form; give your answers as continuous sentences.

5 Express the meaning of the following sentences by using an introductory *it* and an *of* adjunct, e.g. *You are kind to help me.—It is kind of you to help me.* (See the pattern given in the table on p. 114.)

a He was rude to say that.
b I was stupid to forget the tickets.
c That boy is very selfish to take all the sweets and leave none for the rest of us.
d He was cowardly to strike a boy so much smaller than himself.
e You are very good to carry that heavy parcel for me.
f James was mean to refuse to tip the waiter.
g The policeman was kind to help the old lady across the road.
h She is silly to act in that way.
i Your father is very generous to give us all that money to spend.
j Our hostess was very thoughtful to provide us with sandwiches when we left.

B. ACCUSATIVE WITH INFINITIVE: THE INFINITIVE WITH AND WITHOUT *TO*

When the 'accusative with infinitive' construction occurs as the object of a transitive verb, the form of the infinitive generally used is that with *to* prefixed, but there are some verbs which are followed by the infinitive without *to*.

> The teacher made him *repeat* his work. (not *to repeat*)
> I expect them *to arrive* this afternoon. (not *I expect them arrive this afternoon.*)

The student should get to know which verbs belong to which class. The following tables give examples of each type of construction.

VERBS THAT TAKE AN INFINITIVE WITH *TO*

I should *advise* you	to see a doctor.
He would not *allow* us	to see the letter.
I must *ask* you	to refrain from talking.
The prisoner *begged* the judge	to give him another chance.
The bright sunlight *caused* the colour	to fade.
The sentry *commanded* the intruders	to halt.
The bad weather *compelled* us	to stay indoors.
An unexpected legacy *enabled* him	to retire from business.
I *expect* you	to be here by nine o'clock.
I must *get* the joiner	to mend this door.
All his friends *imagined* him	to be well off.
I could not *induce* him	to follow my suggestion.
He *instructed* his bank	not to cash the cheque.
She *liked* her children	to be well dressed.
The highwayman *ordered* the passengers	to hand over their money.
The manager does not *permit* us	to smoke in the office.
Nothing will *persuade* me	to do what I think wrong.
The regulations *require* us	to sign for all books we borrow.
I will *tell* my secretary	to send the letter at once.
I *want* everyone	to listen to this notice.
Your uncle *wishes* you	to telephone him tomorrow.

VERBS THAT TAKE AN INFINITIVE WITHOUT *TO*

They *felt* the floor	vibrate.
I will not *have* my children	misbehave themselves.
We *heard* someone	close a door.
She *lets* her children	have anything they want.
Don't *let* his threats	deter you.
Let us (*Let's*)	go for a walk.
The teacher *made* the pupil	repeat the work.
Did you *notice* anyone	come out of that door?
Several people *saw* the thief	snatch the jewellery.
We *watched* the aeroplane	disappear into the clouds.

Notes

1. When *feel* denotes a feeling of the mind, and is therefore more or less equivalent in meaning to *think*, it takes an infinitive with *to*.

We felt the idea to be a good one.

This construction is confined almost exclusively to the infinitive *to be*.

2. The verbs *know* and *help* may be followed by an infinitive either with or without *to*.

I have never known him (to) lose his temper.
Have you ever known it (to) snow in July?
I helped him (to) mend his bicycle.
Could you help me (to) lift this box, please?

After *help* it is more usual to insert *to* (at least, in British English), and there are still some purists who would insist that it must always be inserted. This may be somewhat pedantic, but even those of us who are more tolerant will probably feel that there are cases where its omission would be unidiomatic. For instance, not many of us would feel it was acceptable English to say:

Writing out a poem will help you learn it.
These tablets will help you sleep.

It is perhaps best for the foreign student always to use the form with *to*, since that is never incorrect.

After *know* it is more usual to omit the *to*, except with the verb *to be* when it denotes the existence of a fact or situation. Thus we should say:

I have never known him be angry with the children.
I have never known him be cruel to animals.

Here *be* refers to a person's attitude, conduct or behaviour, and therefore denotes something akin to an activity. But we could not omit the *to* from such sentences as:

Everyone knew him to be the author of the pamphlet.
I have always known him to be an honest man.

Generally speaking the *to* is not omitted if the infinitive construction could be replaced by a noun clause used as an object.

Everyone knew that he was the author of the pamphlet.

The infinitive after passive verbs

As a general rule a passive verb is followed by the infinitive with *to*, even if the *to* is omitted in the corresponding active form of the sentence.

Active The teacher made him *repeat* his work.
Passive He was made *to repeat* his work. (not *He was made repeat* his work.)
Active The pirate made his victims *walk* the plank.
Passive The pirate's victims were made *to walk* the plank.
Active We heard the teacher *give* the instruction.
Passive The teacher was heard *to give* the instruction.

EXERCISES

1 Complete the following sentences by adding an infinitive or an infinitive followed by other words. (Sometimes an infinitive with *to* will be needed; sometimes one without *to*.)

a No-one heard them .....
b The farmer would not let us .....
c The conductor asked the passengers .....
d We expect the repairs .....
e The children's parents made them .....
f The bandit forced the travellers .....

g The police would not allow anyone .....
h You should not let that dog .....
i They saw two men in dark overcoats .....
j As he left the house he felt something .....
k I like a room....
l The ice on the road caused the car.....
m The manager wants us .....
n As I passed the shop I noticed someone .....
o I never let anyone .....
p The gardener had a boy to help him .....
q That is the first time I have known your father .....
r A spell of fine weather enabled us .....
s I will get my secretary .....
t The two boys watched the car .....
u We have an hour to spare, so let's .....
v Most of us felt the suggestion .....
w The law requires all parents .....
x Can't you persuade your friends ....?
y I do not wish the neighbours .....

2 Compose sentences of your own containing an ' accusative with infinitive ' construction. Use a tense of the following verbs as the finite verbs (one sentence for each verb given):

tell, make, see, order, cause, let, hear, like, forbid, force, help, feel, ask, watch, think.

3 Rewrite the following sentences, using the passive instead of the active voice of the finite verbs.

a I have never known him tell a lie.
b No-one could induce them to accept the offer.
c Their parents did not allow them to play games on a Sunday.
d Someone heard him say that he intended to steal the money.
e The gardener told the boy to sweep up all the dead leaves.
f We saw a small child dash across the road.
g The magistrates made the young hooligans pay for the damage they had done.
h The attendant asked us to return in an hour's time.
i They proved him to be the culprit.
j I expect Mr Brown to be back about 2.30.

C. SOME OTHER POINTS ABOUT THE USE OF THE INFINITIVE

1 The verbs *must*, *may* and *can* are followed by the infinitive without *to*.

> You must work harder.
> The book you are looking for may be in that bookcase.
> I can hear someone coming.

Even when the reference is to the future, it is still the infinitive that is used, not the future tense.

> We must go tomorrow. (not *We must shall go tomorrow.*)
> It may rain this afternoon. (not *It may will rain .....*)
> I can see you in half an hour's time. (not *I can will see you*)

Although all these sentences relate to the future, they express a present possibility or a present sense of obligation.

2 *Ought* is followed by the present infinitive with *to* if it expresses an obligation regarding the present:

> You ought to be ashamed of yourself.

or the future:

> I ought to visit Aunt Mary when I am in London next week.

The same construction may also be used (but only in subordinate clauses) to express an obligation felt in the past:

> I knew I ought to go, though I did not want to.

When the reference is to something that should have been done in the past, but was not done, then *ought* is followed by the perfect infinitive.

> You ought *to have worked* harder. (not *You did ought to work*)
> I ought *to have known* better. (not *I did ought to know*)

3 The verb *know* is never followed by a simple infinitive. If we wish to say that we know the way of doing something, the infinitive must be preceded by *how*.

I know *how* to work that machine. (not *I know to work that machine.*)

The same applies to *tell* and *show* when a way or a method of doing something is concerned

He told me *how* to work the machine.
He showed me *how* to work the machine.

He told me to work the machine would mean that he ordered me to work it.

4 Adjectives such as *easy*, *hard*, *difficult*, *good* and *comfortable*, which denote some quality of a thing or a substance as experienced or appreciated by a person (or by persons in general) are followed by an *active*, not a passive infinitive.

Apples are good *to eat*. (not *to be eaten*)
His speech was difficult *to follow*. (not *to be followed*)

The following table will give you other examples.

I want a book that is easy	to read.
This material is easy	to wash.
These shoes are comfortable	to wear.
Our house is very pleasant	to live in.
Her tale was pitiful	to hear.
That parcel is heavy	to carry.
The destruction was dreadful	to see.
This passage is difficult	to translate.
I found his story hard	to believe.
The consequences of such an act are horrible	to think of.

EXERCISES

1 Complete the following sentences by filling in the blank spaces with the correct part of the verb given in brackets at the end.

a We could not ..... what he said. (hear)
b You must ..... the money by the end of the week. (pay)
c You may ..... when you have finished your work. (go)
d Can you ..... to the concert tonight? (come)
e She felt that she must ..... someone her story. (tell)
f If you are not well you ought ..... a doctor. (see)
g May I ...... another cup of tea, please? (have)

h Must you ..... so soon? (leave)
i Could you ..... me your dictionary for a moment, please? (lend)
j You may ..... my bicycle, if you wish. (borrow)

2 Complete the following sentences by filling in the blank spaces with any suitable verb.

a I am afraid she may ..... ill.
b You ought ..... more attention to your work.
c No-one can ..... the impossible.
d I cannot ..... what this sentence means.
e We must ..... if we wish to catch the train.
f Mary asked her mother whether she might .....
g She was told that she could ..... anyone she liked to the party.
k You ought not .....
i Everyone must ..... if we are to succeed.
j We may not ..... until three o'clock.

3 Complete the following sentences by adding an infinitive construction to denote the way or method of doing something.
e.g. *He asked me.....* *He asked me how to translate the phrase.*

a The pupil asked the teacher .....
b Can you tell me .....?
c John has promised to teach me .....
d You ought to know .....
e No-one could tell us .....
f Only two pupils in the whole class knew .....
g Can anyone tell us .....?
h You will soon learn .....
i We soon found out .....
j The demonstrator explained .....
k The attendant kindly showed us .....
l Is there anyone here who knows .....?

4 Rewrite the following sentences so that they express the idea of something that should have been done but was not.

a You ought to pay that bill.
b He ought not to speak to his elders in that way.
c We ought to start earlier.

d The pupils ought to work harder.
e The shopkeeper ought not to charge so much for that butter.
f I ought to get up earlier.
g Someone ought to tell him of his mistake.
h You ought to stay in bed, with a cold like that.
i We ought to catch an earlier train.
j Oughtn't you to return that book to the library?

5 Complete the following sentences by adding suitable infinitives.

a This word is difficult .....
b This suit is too hot ..... in this warm weather.
c The chair was very comfortable .....
d A dress made of this material is quite easy .....
e Very small objects are hard ......
f Her story was dreadful .....
g This room is not suitable .....
h These berries are not good .....
i That box is too big .....
j His story was interesting .....
k We found the exercise difficult ..... without the help of the teacher.
l The lecture was boring ......, though some of the slides by which it was illustrated were rather interesting.
m The clown was very amusing .....
n The letter was difficult ..... as some of the writing had faded.
o The park is a very pleasant place .....

D. INFINITIVE AND GERUND

1 The gerund is that part of the verb that ends in *-ing* and is used as a verbal noun.

> *Complaining* will not help matters.
> Most boys like *playing* football.
> His chief fault is *idling* his time away.
> The motorist was fined for *exceeding* the speed limit.

In the first sentence the gerund is used as a subject, in the second as an object, in the third as a complement, and in the fourth it is governed by a preposition. It may also stand in apposition to an anticipatory *it*, and may sometimes be used as the ' real ' subject after an introductory *there*.

It is foolish *wasting* your money like that.
There is no *knowing* what may happen.
There's no *pleasing* some people.

2 Some verbs can take either an infinitive or a gerund as an object, but usually there is a slight difference of meaning. The infinitive refers to a specific occasion or a specific instance, whereas the gerund refers to something that is more general.

I do not like *writing* to the newspapers. (A general dislike)
I do not like *to write* to the newspapers. (On a particular occasion or a particular subject)
We prefer *going* by air. (A general preference)
We prefer *to go* by air. (On a particular journey)

With the combination *to be afraid* (*of*), the infinitive denotes the thing that fear inhibits one from doing.

The child was afraid to stroke the dog.
The old lady was afraid to cross the road.

The gerund denotes a possible consequence that causes the fear.

She was afraid of being knocked down by a car.
The child was afraid of being bitten by the dog.

3 The only part of a verb that can follow a preposition is the gerund.

They were punished for *coming* late. (not *for come late*)
The boy was reprimanded for *being* rude to the visitor. (not *for be rude*)

The following is a short table of typical examples, which you should study.

The magistrate fined the motorist	for speeding.
The burglar entered the house	by smashing a window.
She is very clever	at making dresses.
We cannot live	without eating.
I will excuse you	from doing the work.
He was complimented	on winning the prize.
They locked the door	before going out.

Notes

1. It should be unnecessary to point out that sentences such as, *I persuaded him to do it* are not a violation of, or exception to this rule, since *to* is here part of the infinitive, and not a preposition.

2. When it is necessary for an infinitive to follow an expression or a combination of words that normally ends with a preposition, the preposition is dropped.

> Be careful *of* the traffic.
> Be careful *to lock* the safe.

4 From the principle laid down above, it follows that those adjectives and verbs which are always found in combination with a preposition (fond of, interested in, object to) must be followed by the gerund, not by an infinitive, and care must be taken not to omit the preposition.

> I object to doing it. (not *to do it*)
> I am interested in swimming. (not *to swim*)

Similarly compound verbs that end with an adverb (*put off* meaning 'postpone', *keep on* meaning 'continue') take a gerund.

> Although he was very tired, he still kept on *working*. (not *to work*)

The following tables, which give typical examples of each of the three constructions, will be found useful.

ADJECTIVES WITH PREPOSITIONS

I was annoyed at	missing the train.
She is not capable of	doing the work.
We were intent on	achieving our ambition.
Are you interested in	collecting coins?
Who is responsible for	breaking this chair?
We are all tired of	listening to his complaints.
I am not accustomed to	sleeping during the day.
Are you agreeable to	letting them use the car?
These shoes are not suitable for	walking in the country.

VERBS WITH PREPOSITIONS

We aim at	raising five hundred pounds.[1]
I do not agree with	giving waiters tips.
My parents never approved of	playing games on Sunday.
They always disapproved of	playing games on Sunday.
We tried to dissuade him from	doing such a risky thing.
The teacher excused her from	doing the homework.
I insist on	seeing the letter.
Anyone would object to	being cheated of his due.
The accused person persisted in	asserting his innocence.
Illness prevented him from	attending the meeting.
We have succeeded in	gaining our object.[2]
We are thinking of	moving to another house.

VERBS WITH ADVERBS

We must go on	trying.
The snow kept on	falling.
The rude fellow kept on	interrupting us.
I have given up	smoking.
We shall have to put off	going to London.

In the second sentence *kept on* expresses the continuance of something that had been happening before. In the third sentence it expresses repetition or frequency.

Go on may be followed by an infinitive as well as by a gerund, but the meaning is different. *He went on telling us about his schooldays* means that he had been telling us about his schooldays before, and he continued to do so. *He went on to tell us about his schooldays* means that he had been telling us about something else previously, and then, when he had finished that, he continued talking, but on a new subject, his schooldays.

[1] In American English the use of an infinitive after *aim* has long been idiomatic; *We aim to raise five hundred pounds*. Of recent years this has also appeared in British English, and its use is on the increase, but it is still not regarded as strictly correct.

[2] 'Succeed *in doing* something', but 'fail *to do* something'.

VERBS WITHOUT PREPOSITIONS OR ADVERBS

The following verbs do not take a preposition or an adverb, but they must be followed by a gerund, not by an infinitive.

I wanted to avoid	meeting him.
I detest	walking through muddy fields.
Most people dislike	paying taxes.
She enjoys	listening to his stories.
Have you finished	reading that book?
We could not help (prevent ourselves)	hearing what he said.
Do you mind	closing the window?
We must prevent	their coming.
They could not stop	laughing.

EXERCISES

1 Complete the following sentences by inserting in the blank spaces the correct part of the verb given in brackets at the end.

a She was congratulated by her aunt on ..... her examination. (pass)
b The pupils were rebuked for ..... so much noise. (make)
c The prisoner was charged with ..... into a shop. (break)
d This water is not fit for ..... (drink)
e She became ill through ..... too many chocolates. (eat)
f The traveller gave the porter a tip for ..... his luggage. (carry)
g On ..... the news, all the company cheered. (hear)
h By ..... early, they avoided the rush-hour traffic jams. (start)
i We were surprised at ..... so few people there. (find)
j They only managed to finish the task by .... far into the night. (work)
k The candidate was disqualified for .... (cheat)
l Nothing will prevent me from ..... what I think right. (do)
m Where do you think of ..... for your holiday this year? (go)
n Don't let me hinder you from ..... your work. (do)

2 Make the following into sentences by adding a construction with a gerund or an infinitive (whichever you think correct).

a He told the messenger to be careful .....
b My little boy likes .....
c The manager objected .....
d My father was very angry .....
e I do not intend .....
f The inspector is certain .....
g My parents were not accustomed .....
h It would take a good deal to discourage me .....
i Our teacher dislikes .....
j You will succeed if you keep on .....
k He went on ..... as though he did not realise I had entered the room.
l Would you mind .....?
m The mischievous boys tried to annoy the old gentleman .....
n We were very disappointed .....
o She entered the room very quietly, as she was afraid ....
p If there is anything you need, don't be afraid ......
q Most children enjoy .....
r You will never have any money unless you stop .....

3 Explain the difference of meaning between the two sentences in each of the following pairs.

(*a*) She stopped to look in a shop window.
She stopped looking in the shop window.

(*b*) The servant was afraid to disturb his master.
The servant was afraid of disturbing his master.

(*c*) I regret to say he was dishonest.
I regret saying he was dishonest.

(*d*) He gave the man five shillings to wash his car.
He gave the man five shillings for washing his car.

(*e*) He went on speaking of his war experiences.
He went on to speak of his war experiences.

21. Anticipatory *it* with noun clauses and adjective clauses

We have seen on p. 112 that the pronoun *it* may be used as an anticipatory subject in apposition to an infinitive which occurs later in the sentence.

It is wrong to steal.

It is also commonly used in two other types of construction.

1 As an anticipatory subject in apposition to a noun clause which occurs later in the sentence. We do not usually say:

That he will come is unlikely.

Instead we say:

It is unlikely *that he will come.*

(Here the noun clause *that he will come* is in apposition to the anticipatory subject *it.*)

It is believed that the robbery was committed during the night.
It is still not known where they hid the jewels.
It is doubtful whether he ever received the message.

2 As a subject qualified by an adjective clause occurring later in the sentence. We may distinguish two types, and in both *it* may stand not only for a thing, a fact, or a quality, but also for a person.

(*a*) Instead of saying:

The thing that I object to is his rudeness.

or

The person who made the discovery was the village policeman.

we may say:

It is his rudeness that I object to.
It was the village policeman that (or *who*) made the discovery.

(*b*) Instead of saying:

The lane that has no turning is a long lane.

or

The father that knows his own child is a wise father.

we say:

It's a long lane that has no turning.
It's a wise father that knows his own child.

In this second type the pronoun *it* stands for, and anticipates, the noun that follows as the complement of the verb. In both types the adjective clause qualifies *it*, not the noun by which it is immediately preceded, but the verb of the adjective clause takes its person and number from the preceding noun or pronoun.

It is I who *am* to blame.
It is the children who *are* likely to be most interested.

EXERCISES

1 Rewrite the following sentences using the anticipatory *it* as the subject.

a That we shall have to do the work ourselves is obvious.
b That you were unable to come to the party is a pity.
c Whether we shall be able to go is uncertain.
d That we cannot rely on his help is obvious.
e That he should behave in that way is disgraceful.
f Why she did it is not known.
g What caused the fire has not yet been discovered.
h That he is a millionaire is said by some people.
i That we came just too late was unfortunate.
j That the thieves were still in the building was never suspected.

2 Express the ideas in the following sentences by using the construction with an anticipatory *it* qualified by an adjective clause.

a The heart that never rejoices is a poor heart.
b The thing that ruined him was gambling.
c The wind that blows no-one any good is an ill wind.
d The person who gave the secret away was Smith.

e The person who is responsible for the mistake is myself.
f The thing that killed him was drink.
g The people that amused the children most were the clowns.
h The thing that amazes me is the daring of the fellow.
i The person who won the prize was George, not Eric.
j Who was the person who said, ' The child is father of the man '?

22. The position of adverbs

1 Adverbs of frequency (always, often, rarely, never, ever, generally, usually, sometimes, occasionally). If the verb is a simple tense form, the adverb is normally placed between the subject and the verb, except when the verb is some part of *to be*; then the adverb follows the verb.

We *always* walk to school.
I *often* met your cousin when I was in Hong Kong.
My sister *never* drinks tea.
If you *ever* come to Brighton, call and see me.

But:

He is *never* late.
The train is *always* punctual.
Elderly people are *often* deaf.
If you are *ever* in difficulties, seek expert advice.
I am *usually* at the office by nine o'clock.

If the verb form is a compound one, the adverb is placed after the auxiliary, and if the auxiliary is itself a compound form, after the first word of the auxiliary.

I shall *never* forget this occasion. (not *I shall forget never* ....)
We have *usually* finished our work by four o'clock.
He has *always* been rather lazy.
Our team has *never* been beaten.
Serious accidents have *sometimes* been caused by thoughtlessness.

The verbs *can*, *could*, *may*, *might*, *must* and *ought* are treated as auxiliaries; the adverb of frequency comes between these words and the infinitive.

> One ought *always* to be honest.
> We may *never* see such a sight again.
> You must *always* take care when crossing a busy road.
> I can *usually* tell whether a person is lying or not.

In negative sentences the adverb of frequency follows the word *not*.

> I have not *always* been deaf.
> He is not *often* late.
> It is not *usually* as cold as this in July.
> Railway porters don't *generally* refuse a tip.

In interrogative sentences (where inversion of verb and subject occurs), the adverb of frequency follows immediately after the subject.

> Do you *often* go bathing?
> Has your brother *never* written to you?
> Is the High Street *always* as busy as this?
> Have you *ever* ridden on an elephant?
> Isn't there *usually* a queue at the bus stop?

Not all the adverbs of frequency can be used with an imperative, but those that can are placed immediately before the verb, in the same way as they are for a positive statement that uses a simple tense form.

> Always be truthful.
> Never buy what you cannot pay for.

N.B. The rules given above refer to the general practice, and unless he is very proficient in English the student had better follow these. Occasionally, however, and for special purposes, the adverb may be found in a different place. In particular the following should be noticed.

(*a*) *Often* may be placed at the end of the sentence if we wish to emphasise it. This occurs most frequently in negative statements and in questions, much less frequently in positive statements.

I don't see him *often*, as we live a long way from each other.
Do you come here *often?*

(*b*) *Never* is sometimes placed at the beginning of the sentence in order to emphasise it; but in that case the verb and subject that follow are inverted in order, as they would be for a question.

I never saw such a sight.
Never did I see such a sight.
I have never known such a cold summer.
Never have I known such a cold summer.

(*c*) In conditional clauses *ever* sometimes follows immediately after *if;* but this is probably because the two are felt to form a compound expressive of a single idea, rather like *whenever* and *wherever*.

If ever I become rich I will found a fund to help poor teachers of English.

2 *Still* and *just* (the latter, when it denotes time) follow the same rules as the adverbs of frequency; but *even* and *only* must be attached to the word they modify, according to the idea that the sentence is intended to express.

Even a child could do that. (i.e., so young and inexperienced a person as a child)
He escaped without *even* a scratch. (i.e., so slight an injury as a scratch)
He *even* robbed his parents. (i.e., in addition to other misdeeds)
He robbed *even* his parents. (i.e., in addition to robbing other people)
Only you know the answer. (i.e., you and no-one else)
I *only* pretended to be ill. (i.e., if the stress is on *pretended*, I was not really ill; if the stress is on *only*, all I did was to pretend to be ill.)
I saw her *only* yesterday. (i.e., as recently as yesterday)
Admission will be by ticket *only*. (i.e., and by no other means)
She is *only* six years old. (i.e., six and no more)

3 Adverbs and adverbial expressions denoting place, time, or duration of time, generally go either at the beginning or at the end of the sentence (or of the clause in a complex sentence).

> At the cross-roads they came to a halt.
> They came to a halt at the cross-roads.
> In the room were two people.
> There were two people in the room.
> Every evening we go for a walk.
> We go for a walk every evening.
> For two hours they did not stir.
> They did not stir for two hours.

When the adverbial expression is placed at the beginning, more prominence or more emphasis is given to it. Sometimes its position is determined by what has gone before, in the previous sentence.

> A car was standing at the side of the road. In it were two men.

It would not be ungrammatical to say *Two men were in it*, but it is more natural to put *in it* first because the end of the last sentence has centred our attention on the car, and so we start the next sentence from that point.

With imperatives, the normal place of adverbial expressions of time and place is after the verb.

> Come back at three o'clock.
> Don't worry about that now.
> Meet me opposite the Town Hall.

But they are sometimes found before the verb, especially when the imperative is employed to give directions to people (i.e., to instruct them in how to do something).

> Take a saucepan, and *into it* pour half a pint of milk.
> *Just past the church* take the turning to the right.
> *During cold weather* keep the plants indoors.

The front position of the adverbial expression draws special attention to it.

EXERCISES

1 Insert *always*, *ever*, *never*, *usually*, *often*, *seldom* or *sometimes* in the following sentences. Make sure you put the adverb in the right place.

a You should show respect to your elders.
b No-one has been to Mars.
c It is too late to mend.
d We spend the week-end in the country.
e Even the most careful person can make a mistake.
f I go to see my uncle, as the journey is so difficult.
g You can trust a person who is dishonest.
h I get up at seven o'clock.
i Have you lived in this house?
j Have you been to Paris?
k Is the room any warmer than this?
l A bully is a person of much courage.

2 Insert *still* or *just* in the correct places in the following sentences.

a The train has left.
b It is raining.
c Is your son at school?
d My brother has got a new job.
e I do not understand the question.
f I have been told an astonishing piece of news.
g She insisted that she had never seen the person before.
h Though it was May the evenings were rather chilly.
i A party of travellers had arrived at the hotel.
j Have you finished that novel yet? No, I am reading it.
k Is the shop open?
l No, it has closed.
m He was leaving the house when the telephone bell rang.
n Do you need my help?
o He has paid me ten pounds, but he owes me another five. (Use both *still* and *just* in this sentence.)

3 Rewrite the following sentences to bring out the same meaning by using *only*. See that you put the word in the correct place; e.g. *He had a pound and no more in his possession.—He had only a pound in his possession.*

a An expert, and no-one else, could do that.
b It was as recently as a week ago that I was speaking to him.
c When I said that, I was joking, that is all.
d No more than two pupils could answer the question.
e We have five minutes, and no more, in which to catch the train.
f This ticket is valid for one month, and for no longer.
g I have glanced at the letter; I have not read it thoroughly.
h No-one but a fool would waste his money like that.
i Some of those rescued from the fire had their night-clothes on, and nothing else.
j It was by nothing but an accident that the mistake was discovered.

4 Add to the following sentences suitable adverbs or adverbial expressions of either time or place.

a I cannot see you.
b Be at the station.
c The weather has been fine.
d That child has been crying.
e We ate our meal.
f A serious accident occurred.
g The miser hid his gold.
h We stayed indoors.
i Several spectators fainted.
j A splendid view can be seen.

23. Verbs compounded with adverbs: the position of the object

A number of verbs in English are often followed by an adverb, and the two words together make what is virtually a compound verb expressive of a single idea (put on, take off, lay down, give up, make up, put out). When such verbs are used transitively, if the object is a noun, it can usually be placed either immediately before or immediately after the adverb.

> When you enter a house you should *take off your hat.*
> When you enter a house you should *take your hat off.*
> It took us a long time to *make up our minds.*
> It took us a long time to *make our minds up.*
> Have you all *given your homework in*?
> Have you all *given in your homework*?

But if the object is a personal pronoun, it can be placed only *before* the adverb.

> If you have your hat on, *take it off.* (not *take off it*)
> *Ring me up* at 3.30. (not *Ring up me*)
> When you have thought of the answer, *write it down.* (not *write down it*)
> The blow almost *knocked him out.* (not *knocked out him*)

The demonstrative pronouns *this*, *that*, *these* and *those* may occupy either position, according to the word that the speaker wishes to emphasise, the emphasis falling on the word that comes at the end.

> Take this down. (Here the speaker wishes to emphasise the fact that the students are to take down what he is saying, and not merely listen to it, so he puts *down* at the end of the sentence.)
> Take down this. (Here the students, who are waiting to take down something, are told what they are to take down, so *this* is the important word, and is placed at the end of the sentence.)

Notes

1. When the object is a noun the position is often determined by considerations of emphasis. A speaker wishing to make a count, and asking for a show of hands, will probably say:

> If you wish to join the party, put up your hands.

When he has made his count he will probably say:

> You may put your hands down now.

as he wishes to emphasise the word *down.*

2. A long object (e.g. a noun with qualifying words attached to it) usually goes after the adverb.

> The students took down everything the teacher told them.

To say *The students took everything the teacher told them down* would place the adverb so far away from its verb that the sentence would sound awkward.

If, on the other hand, the adverb has other words attached to it, the object will probably precede it, otherwise it would be too far separated from the verb to which it is the object.

> He threw down the book
> or
> He threw the book down.

But:

> He threw the book down on the floor.

We could not say:

> He threw down on the floor the book
> or
> He threw down the book on the floor.

3. There are a number of words which can be used as both adverbs and prepositions. It is important for the student to distinguish between an adverb followed by an object, and the same word used as a preposition to introduce a phrase. In both cases it will be followed by a noun or a pronoun, but the preposition cannot change places with the noun as the adverb can.

> He turned down the page.

Here *down* is an adverb, and the sentence can be changed to:

> He turned the page down.

But now look at this sentence:

> The ink ran down the page.

Here *down* is a preposition introducing the adverb phrase *down the page* and the order of the words in this phrase cannot be changed. We cannot say:

> The ink ran the page down.

We can generally distinguish the two constructions in this way: if the verb is transitive before any word is added to it, then the word with which we are concerned is an adverb;

if the verb is intransitive, then the word with which we are concerned is a preposition. Thus in the sentence *He turned down the page*, *turned* is a transitive verb, with *the page* as its object. Hence *down* is an adverb. But in *The ink ran down the page*, *ran* is an intransitive verb; hence *down* is a preposition.

There are, however, certain combinations like *to look after*, *to look at*, *to look for*, *to care for*, *to deal with*, which have the force of transitive verbs, though they are actually made up of an intransitive one followed by a preposition. In such combinations, of course, the two words must always stand together; first, because only when they are together do they make sense; and secondly because the second word of the combination, being a preposition (though it is no longer felt to introduce a phrase), cannot be shifted in any case.

EXERCISES

1 Complete the following sentences by inserting in the correct places the verb and adverb given at the end of each one. Only one space is indicated in each sentence, but this does not necessarily mean that both words are to go in the space. In some cases both may go there, but in others only the verb will go there and the adverb will be placed after the object. You must use your judgment.

a The cyclist ..... a pedestrian. (knocked down)
b If you don't get out of my way, I'll ..... you. (knock down)
c You are to ..... the whole of this exercise. (write out)
d When you ..... it, make sure there are no mistakes in it. (have written out)
e No-one could .... the answer to the question. (find out)
f I'm not going to tell you the answer; you must .....it for yourself. (find out)
g If you don't know how to spell a word, ... it in a dictionary. (look up)
h The constable ..... in his note book the information which the witness gave him. (took down)
i She ..... the letter and threw the pieces on the fire. (tore up)
j Get the books from the cupboard and ..... them to the pupils. (give out)
k In order to apply for a ticket you must ..... a form. (fill in)

l When she had put the letter in the envelope she ..... it. (sealed up)
m The cashier slowly ..... the money. (counted out)
n He ..... a cheque for a hundred pounds. (wrote out)
o These figures are needed for a very important purpose, so see that you ..... them correctly. (add up)

2 Where possible, change the position of the italicised word in each of the following sentences. If it is not possible to change it, explain why.

a The teacher told the pupils to put *down* their pens.
b The firemen quickly put *out* the fire.
c The writing on the blackboard is needed for next lesson, so don't rub it *out*.
d The servant brought *in* the coffee.
e She put some sugar *in* the coffee.
f Write *down* all the particulars that I shall dictate to you.
g As the time is inconvenient we shall have to put the meeting *off*.
h An announcer called *out* the names of those who had won prizes.
i He put his hand *in* his pocket and took *out* some money.
j We invited the stranger *in*.

24. Tag questions

Tag questions are questions attached to the end of a statement in order to draw attention to it or to give it added force. Although they nominally ask the opinion of the person to whom they are addressed, they do not really do so; they take his agreement for granted. They are used only in conversation and in letters between friends where the writer adopts the same kind of style that he would use if he were actually speaking to his correspondent. It is important that the student should learn the correct use of them. The chief points to notice are as follows.

1 A positive statement takes a negative tag, and a negative statement takes a positive tag.

> It *is* very cold today, *isn't it*?
> It is *not* very warm today, *is it*?
> We *have* plenty of time, *haven't we*?
> We *hadn't* much time, *had we*?

A negative statement does not necessarily mean one with a negative verb. It may have a positive verb, with a negative subject, object or complement, or a negative adverb that modifies the verb. So long as there is a *negative idea* in it, it is a negative statement, and needs a positive tag.

> *None* of the food was wasted, *was it*?
> We saw *no-one* we knew, *did we*?
> A small scratch like that is *nothing*, *is it*?
> Money goes *nowhere* nowadays, *does it*?

2 Semi-negative or depreciative words like *little*, *few*, *hardly*, *scarcely*, *rarely*, *seldom* are treated as negatives, and take a positive tag.

> Few people knew the answer, did they?
> Little progress has been made, has it?
> We could scarcely hear what he said, could we?
> We seldom see them nowadays, do we?

Notes

Though *few* and *little* are negative, *a few* and *a little* are positive, and therefore need a negative tag.

> A few people knew the answer, didn't they?
> A little progress has been made, hasn't it?

The adverb *only* may take either a positive or a negative tag.

> There were only six people present, were there?
> There were only six people present, weren't there?

The positive tag implies an attempt to verify the information. Only the negative tag implies that the agreement of the person addressed is taken for granted.

3 If a personal pronoun is the subject of the statement, then this same personal pronoun is repeated as the subject of the tag; so is the formal subject *there*. But if a noun or any pronoun other than a personal one is the subject of the statement, the tag has *he*, *she*, *it* or *they*. The generalising personal pronoun *one* in the statement must be followed by *one* in the tag, not by *he*, *they* or *you*.

> *He* is very clever, isn't *he*?
> *That girl* isn't very attractive, is *she*?
> *One* can't be too careful, can *one*?

4 If the verb of the statement is a simple tense form of *to be* or *to have* (the latter when it denotes possession or some idea closely related to possession), this tense is also used in the tag. (Though remember that the interrogative form of *I am not* is *aren't I*? See p. 77)

> John has a bad cold, hasn't he?
> I'm older than you, aren't I?

If it is a simple tense of any other verb, or of the verb *have* denoting something other than possession, it is represented in the tag by *do* or *did*.

> She looks ill, doesn't she?
> We have breakfast at eight o'clock, don't we?

Used to also uses *do* or rather the past tense of it, *did*.

> She used to be quite a good tennis player, didn't she?

5 If the verb of the statement is a compound tense, then only the auxiliary (or, if the auxiliary itself is a compound form, only the first word of it) is repeated in the tag. For these purposes *can*, *may*, *must*, *ought* and the anomalous *need* are treated as auxiliaries.

> We have finished our work, haven't we?
> They haven't paid for their seats, have they?
> Your car is being repaired, isn't it?
> You can be drowned in a few inches of water, can't you?
> We mustn't be late, must we?

6 Imperative verbs are a class apart. If they are simple requests, they usually take *will you*?, no matter what the verb and no matter whether it is a positive or negative request.

Pass me the newspaper, *will you*, please.
Don't be late for dinner, *will you?*

If they are invitations or suggestions, they may also take *will you?* but *won't you?* is used to give urgency.

Have another cup of tea, will you?
Have another cup of tea, won't you?

Since *won't you* suggests urgency, it is the form of the tag used with entreaties, or requests that have the force of entreaties.

Be careful when you cross the road, won't you?
Remember to lock the door, won't you?

A suggestion that uses *let's* (short for *let us*) uses *shall we?* in the tag.

Let's have a game of cricket, shall we?

An imperative that expresses impatience or that has the force of a rebuke, uses *can't you?* as the tag.

Use your common sense, can't you?

Notes

1. Although *everybody* and *everyone*, are singular, for the purposes of the tag they are usually treated as plural, and referred to by *they*.

Everybody can't come in first, can they?
Everyone cheered wildly, didn't they?

2. *None of*, followed by a plural noun, is also treated as a plural, and takes *they*.

None of the workmen arrived to time, did they?

3. *None of us* has *we* as the subject of the tag.

None of us knew the way, did we?

Some of us takes *we* if the speaker includes himself in the number, but *they* if he does not.

Some of us wanted to stay longer, didn't we?
On the return journey some of us lost the way, didn't they?

Some of you takes *you* in the tag.

Some of you are learning Russian, aren't you?

EXERCISES

Add the appropriate tag to the following sentences. (Remember that when you add the tag the existing full stop must be changed to a comma.)

1. We haven't had our lunch yet.
2. We were only just in time.
3. The car broke down at a most awkward time.
4. Everyone is liable to make mistakes.
5. She will miss the train if she doesn't hurry.
6. The garden looks very attractive.
7. The journey was not an easy one.
8. The attendant would not let us in.
9. I never drink tea.
10. The hotel was not too expensive.
11. Let's go and see their new house.
12. He easily loses his temper.
13. Elephants are very strong animals.
14. There was not a single seat vacant.
15. We mustn't forget to pay for our tickets.
16. You needn't leave so early as this.
17. See that the safe is securely locked.
18. We hadn't much time to spare.
19. No-one could tell us the way to the station.
20. Your father mightn't like us to use his new typewriter.
21. That was not a very polite thing to say.
22. Most of us voted against the proposal.
23. There's no sense in wasting one's money.
24. Our team hasn't been beaten all this season.
25. We could go for a trip round the world if we had the money.
26. Let's go for a swim.
27. Sit in this more comfortable chair.
28. There won't be time to get lunch before the lecture.
29. The house needs re-painting.
30. We shall have to start early.

25. Appended questions

What we call 'appended questions' resemble tag questions in that they are attached to the end of a statement; but they are used for a different purpose. We may distinguish three types.

1 Those that ask for confirmation of the statement.

> You will be nineteen on your next birthday, won't you?
> Your father used to be Principal of the Technical College, didn't he?
> The bus does not leave until 10.45, does it?
> The rent is not due until the end of the month, is it?

The rules for this type are the same as those for tag questions. But when the statement consists of more than one clause, the question uses the subject and verb appropriate to those in the clause containing what is to be confirmed.

> I believe you are just eighteen years old, aren't you? (not *don't I?*)

2 Those that hope for a denial of a negative statement that precedes them.

> You didn't happen to notice the time when we passed that clock, did you?
> You couldn't lend me half a crown, could you?
> You haven't seen my purse lying about anywhere, have you?
> This isn't all the bread we have, is it?

Sentences of this type, as the second example will show, are often an indirect way of making a request which the speaker feels reluctant to make more directly. The rules are the same as for the tag question, except that, again, where the statement consists of more than one clause the question uses the subject and verb appropriate to those in the clause containing the assertion which it is hoped will be denied.

> I suppose you couldn't lend me half a crown, could you? (not *don't I?*)

3 Those that are attached to a statement (either positive or negative) of the speaker's position or opinion, and then ask for that of the person addressed.

> I didn't care for that film, did you?
> I can't understand why he did it, can you?
> I think we ought to be going now, don't you?

The rules for the verb are the same as those for the tag questions, but the subject is always *you*. And of course, the particular verb form that goes with *you* must be used, if it differs from that used in the statement.

> I *shouldn't* be surprised if it rained tomorrow, *would* you? (not *should you?*)

EXERCISES

1 Add to the following statements an appended question, either asking for confirmation or inviting denial.

a I believe you have two brothers.
b Your father has retired from business.
c You wouldn't care to come to the theatre with us.
d I think I have lent you this book before.
e You are not going out in that shabby old suit.
f *Paradise Lost* was written by John Milton.
g He lived in the seventeenth century.
h Now your son has got a new bicycle he doesn't want to sell his old one.
i They haven't lived here very long.
j We needn't pay the money until we receive the goods.

2 Add to the following sentences an appended question asking the other person's opinion.

a I don't think much of that picture.
b I should like to go to America one day.
c I feel ready for a cup of tea.
d I can hear someone singing.
e I wasn't very interested in his story.
f I shan't give anything to the fund.
g I couldn't hear what he was saying.

h I think Jane looks very tired.
i I have never been to Spain.
j I don't like paying more for a thing than it's really worth.

26. Indirect (reported) questions

The points to remember about indirect questions are the following.

1 The inversion of verb and subject that occurs in direct questions does not take place in indirect. The order is the same as that for statements: subject then verb.

Direct Question	Where is your book?
Indirect Question	Tell me *where your book is.* (not .....*where is your book.*)
	He asked me where my book was. (not.....*where was my book.*)

2 If the expected answer to the question could be either *yes* or *no*, then the indirect form is introduced by *whether*.

Direct Question	Are you going to the party?
Indirect Question	Ask him *whether* he is going to the party. (not.....*is he going to the party.*)

N.B. *If* is sometimes used instead of *whether*. It would be quite correct, for instance, to say:

Ask him if he is going to the party.

But *if* cannot be used with all verbs, and unless the student is certain that it is suitable he had better avoid it. *Whether* is always correct.

3 As indirect questions have the same subject-verb order as statements, they use the same form of the verb . For the past and present tenses, most English verbs use *do* or *did* in the interrogative forms (i.e., for direct questions), but these are not used in *positive* indirect questions, because they are not used in the corresponding positive statements.

Statement	He likes coffee.
Direct Question	Do you like coffee?
Indirect Question	Ask him whether he likes coffee.

(not *whether he does like coffee*, or *does he like coffee*.)

She asked him whether he liked coffee.
(not *whether he did like coffee*, or *did he like coffee*.)

But *do* and *did* are used in the corresponding *negative* indirect questions, because they are used in negative statements.

Negative Statement	I don't like coffee.
Direct Question	Don't you like coffee?
Indirect Question	Ask him why he doesn't like coffee.
	She asked him why he didn't like coffee.

There are, however, a few verbs that do not use *do* and *did* in negative statements (*have* when it denotes possession, *be*, *can*, *must*, *may*, *ought*) and these do not use them either in negative indirect questions.

I wonder why he isn't here.
The inspector asked us why we hadn't a ticket.
I don't know why they can't get here earlier.

4 An indirect question is not enclosed in inverted commas (quotation marks), and it does not have a question mark at the end. But a question mark is necessary if the whole sentence in which the indirect question is included is itself a direct question.

Did you remember to ask when the train arrived?

The indirect question *When the train arrived* does not itself need a question mark, but one has to be used because the whole sentence, which starts with *Did you remember?* is a question. If the whole question were reported, so that the present main clause became a subordinate one, then the question mark would not be used.

He inquired whether I remembered to ask when the train arrived.

EXERCISES

1 Change the following direct questions into indirect questions by adding a suitable main clause to them and making any other necessary alterations.

a Do you think it will rain?
b When does your brother return from England?
c How does this machine work?
d When do you take up your new post?
e Shall I close the window?
f Where did you go for your holiday?
g Who lives in that large house at the corner?
h Why is that child crying?
i How many English lessons do you have each week?
j Could I borrow your bicycle?
k Do you find English a difficult language to learn?
l How many brothers and sisters have you?
m Is the train likely to be late?
n How long have you been learning English?
o Need you work so late?
p Are you going to take an examination in English?
q Why was Mr Brown late for work this morning?
r Have you written to your aunt to thank her for your present?
s What must I do to get a seat for the play?
t When shall I know the result of the examination?

2 Give an answer to each of the questions in the previous exercise, in the form of a direct statement.

3 Make up five sentences of your own in which an indirect question is included. The indirect questions should start with the following words: (*a*) when, (*b*) where, (*c*) whether, (*d*) why, (*e*) how.

27. The indirect expression of imperatives

There are two ways of expressing imperatives in the indirect form.

1 By a noun clause expressed as an indirect statement and containing a verb such as *is to*, *are to* or *must*, which expresses obligation (or, in the negative, prohibition).

2 By an accusative noun or pronoun denoting the person who is to comply with the command, instruction or request, followed by an infinitive denoting the action.

Imperative	Keep the gate closed.
Indirect Form	He told them that they were to keep the gate closed.
	He told them they must keep the gate closed.
	He told them to keep the gate closed.
Imperative	Don't tease that dog.
Indirect Form	He told them that they were not to tease the dog.
	He told them that they must not tease the dog.
	He told them not to tease the dog.

Tell, as will be seen from the examples above, can take both constructions, but *say* can take only the noun clause, while *ask*, *implore*, *entreat*, *order* and *command* can take only the accusative followed by the infinitive.

He says that we are to keep the gate closed.
(not *He says us to keep the gate closed*, or *He says to keep the gate closed.*)
He asked us to keep the gate closed.
(not *He asked that we were to keep the gate closed.*)[1]

[1] It is possible to say '*He asked that we should keep the gate closed*', but this is a rather different kind of noun clause from the others; and in any case it does not really represent an indirect form of an imperative. Rather it is a paraphrase of the substance of what might have been an imperative request.

Thus the negative imperative *Don't touch those papers* may be rendered in the indirect form in one or other of the following ways.

> He says that we are not to touch these papers.
> He asks us not to touch these papers.

The one we should use in a particular instance depends on the idea we wish to convey. *Ask* suggests a request; *says* suggests a prohibition.

When an imperative gives advice rather than a command or an instruction, the noun clause uses *should* instead of *is to*, *are to*, or *must*.

> Never live beyond your means.
> He told us that we should never live beyond our means.
> Always take heed of good advice.
> He told us that we should always take heed of good advice.

The accusative followed by the infinitive may also be used for this purpose.

> He told us (*or* warned us) never to live beyond our means.
> He told us always to take heed of good advice.

Note that adverbs like *not*, *never*, *always* must be placed before the *to* of the infinitive. It would be incorrect to say:

> to *never* live beyond our means
> to *always* take heed of good advice
> to *not* touch these papers

These are examples of the mistake known as the split infinitive.

EXERCISES

1 Express the following imperative sentences in the indirect form, using as the verb of the main clause that given in brackets at the end of the sentence.

a Make less noise. (tell)
b Open the window, please. (ask)
c Don't walk on the grass. (say)
d Meet me at 3.30. (ask)

e Write the exercise for homework. (tell)
f Stand up when the inspector enters. (say)
g Don't tell anyone the secret. (say)
h Pass me the sugar, please Susan. (ask)
i Turn to page 25 in your grammar books. (tell)
j Do stay a little longer. (entreat)
k Find Mr Smith and give him this message. (ask)
l Read through your work when you have finished it. (say)

2 Express the following imperative sentences in the indirect form. In the main clause use whichever verb you think is the most suitable.

a Pick up all that paper from the floor.
b Don't leave the office until I return.
c Find out what time the train starts.
d Give me another chance.
e Always be polite when you speak to people.
f Never cross the road without first looking to see that it is clear.
g Don't be cross with the children.
h Let me have a look at that letter.
i Leave this room instantly.
j Put these papers on my desk.
k Do tell us a story, grandpa.[1]
l Hand over your money.

28. The use of correlatives

There are certain conjunctions or conjunctive expressions in English that always go in pairs. These are known as correlatives. The chief ones are: *either.....or*, *neither.....nor*, *both.....and*, *not only ..... but also*. Care is needed in their use. The points to remember about them are the following.

[1] *Grandpa* is a childish word for *grandfather*.

1 The second of each pair must always be the complementary one to the first: *either* must be followed by *or* (not by *nor*), and conversely *neither* must be followed by *nor* (not by *or*).

He is *neither* willing *nor* capable. (not *or capable*)

2 Care must be taken to see that the correlatives are placed in the correct positions in the sentence. The general rule is that all words that refer to both alternatives must be placed before the first of the correlatives.

The following is incorrect:

You may either have an apple or an orange.

The two alternatives are (*a*) You may have an apple; (*b*) You may have an orange. The words common to both are *You may have;* these must therefore go before the first of the correlatives, and the correct version of the sentence is:

You may have *either* an apple *or* an orange.

Here are some further examples.

Wrong He not only cheated his friends, but also his parents.
Right He cheated not only his friends, but also his parents.
Wrong She neither cares for gold nor silver.
Right She cares for neither gold nor silver.
Wrong The elephant both swallowed the bag and the buns.
Right The elephant swallowed both the bag and the buns.

These may be set out in tabular form as follows.

Words in Common	First Alternative	Second Alternative
He is	neither willing	nor capable.
You may have	either an apple	or an orange.
He cheated	not only his friends	but also his parents.
She cares for	neither gold	nor silver.
The elephant swallowed	both the bag	and the buns.

Note

We have said above that the *general* rule is that all words that refer to both alternatives are placed before the first of the correlatives. But there are two exceptions.

1. *Infinitives* The word *to* cannot be detached from the rest of an infinitive. The two count together as one word. Hence when the two correlated terms begin with an infinitive, each must retain its *to*, and the first correlative must go before the *to* of the first infinitive. To place it after the *to* would be to commit the mistake of the split infinitive, referred to on p. 151.

> The shopkeeper offered to exchange the goods. The shopkeeper offered to refund the money.

When these two sentences are combined they will become,

> The shopkeeper offered *either* to exchange the goods, *or* to refund the money. (not *to either exchange the goods or refund the money.*)

2. *Prepositions* When a preposition is felt to belong to the verb which precedes it, the two together making a compound transitive verb, it goes with its verb before the first of the correlatives and is omitted from the two correlated terms.

> She cared for the sick. (*care for=tend*) She cared for the wounded.
> She cared for *both* the sick *and* the wounded.

But when the two correlated terms are phrases that both begin with the same preposition, each usually retains its own preposition, since a phrase is equivalent to a single part of speech (an adjective or an adverb) and without its preposition it is felt to be incomplete.

> You may put the books on the shelf. You may put the books on the desk.

Strictly speaking, the words that these two sentences have in common are *You may put the books on;* but *on* does not count, because it forms part of two different phrases (*on the shelf*, *on the desk*).

The correlated form will therefore become,

> You may place the books *either* on the shelf *or* on the desk. (not *You may place the books on either the shelf or the desk.*)

EXERCISES

Express in one sentence the ideas contained in the following pairs of sentences, by using correlatives.

1. He is not honest. He is not truthful.
2. You may have a camera for your birthday. You may have a watch for your birthday. (Express these as alternatives.)
3. We shall go by bus. We shall go by train. (Express these as alternatives.)
4. He sold the land. He sold the house.
5. The old man could not read. The old man could not write.
6. The thieves stole the jewels. The thieves smashed up part of the interior of the shop.
7. You must pay for the goods. You must return them. (Express as alternatives.)
8. The driver was killed. His passenger was killed.
9. The driver was not injured. His passenger was not injured.
10. I am willing to meet you in Manchester. I am willing to meet you in Liverpool. (Express as alternatives.)
11. They did not know where they had come from. They did not know where they were going.
12. She has lost her purse. She has lost her handbag.

29. *Who* and *whom*

1 Use *who* for the subject of a verb, and *whom* for the object, or when it is the object of a preposition.

> *Who* told you that story? (subject)
> This is the person *who* brought the message. (subject)
> He is a person *whom* everyone likes. (object)
> What is the name of that person to *whom* you were speaking? (object of a preposition)

But if the preposition comes at the end of the sentence or clause, then use *who*.

Who is that letter from? (not *whom*)
Who did you give it to? (not *whom*)

N.B. This is always the spoken form; but in more formal English we should say:

To whom did you give it?

2 Care must be taken, however, when the preposition governs a whole clause that begins with *who* (or *whom*), and not merely the pronoun itself. In such cases, whether we use *who* or *whom* depends on the function of the word in its own clause; it has nothing to do with the preposition that precedes it.

It all depends on *who* comes. (Here *who* is used because it is the subject of *comes*.)
It all depends on *whom* you ask. (Here *whom* is used because it is the object of *ask*.)

EXERCISES

Complete the following sentences by inserting *who* or *whom* in the blank spaces.

1. He is a person ..... everyone admires.
2. I don't mind ..... you ask to the party.
3. Do you know .... was responsible for the damage?
4. ..... was the letter addressed to?
5. Always see that those with ..... you associate are of good character.
6. ..... do you think we should invite?
7. Whether I will join the party depends on ..... is organising it.
8. He is not a person ..... I would trust.
9. ..... was that dark-haired person you were sitting with?
10. This is not the waitress ..... served us the last time we were here.
11. Do you know ..... that man in the grey suit is?
12. ..... did you mean, when you referred to 'a certain person ..... everyone knows'?

13. I cannot bear people ..... are always complaining of their misfortunes.
14. One of the people with ..... I work has just won a large sum of money in a lottery.
15. I cannot remember ..... I lent my English dictionary to.
16. ..... I choose to have as my friends is nothing to do with you.
17. Everyone ..... heard him speak agreed that he was a great orator.
18. I shall give the money to ..... I like.
19. He is a man of great experience, from ..... much can be learned.
20. Do you know ..... was the author of the novel *Lorna Doone*?

30. *Much* and *many*

When used as an adjective or a pronoun, *much* refers to amount or quanity, and *many* to number. That is to say, *many* is used for countables, and *much* for non-countables.

> *Many* of my friends are learning English.
> Were *many* houses damaged by the gale?
> *Many* of us thought the examination difficult.
> *Much* of the land is uncultivated.
> We have not *much* food left.
> How *much* money will you need?

Both *much* and *many* have as their comparative and superlative degrees, *more* and *most*.

> Many people—more people—most people
> Much of the land—more of the land—most of the land

EXERCISES

Supply *much* or *many* to fill the blank spaces in the following sentences.

1. We have not had ..... wet days this month.
2. Have you read ..... English poems?
3. I haven't ..... opportunity for study during the day.

4. ..... people were made homeless by the floods.
5. They lost ..... of their property.
6. She could not feel ..... sympathy for a person who had come to grief through his own stupidity.
7. We have not had ..... to eat.
8. ..... of the eggs were broken.
9. We have walked ..... miles today.
10. Not ..... people could afford to buy so expensive a car as that.
11. ..... of what he said was nonsense.
12. The medicine did not do him ..... good.
13. She did not make ..... mistakes in her essay.
14. ..... of the passengers had a narrow escape.
15. We found the house without ..... difficulty.

31. *Much* and *very*

1 *Very* is used to modify adjectives and adverbs of the positive degree, *much* to modify those of the comparative degree.

This room is *very* large.
This room is *much* larger than the other.
He drives *very* carefully.
He drives *much* more carefully than he used to.

2 *Much* is also used to modify participles when they have their full verbal function. (*Very* can never be used for this purpose.)

This question has been *much* discussed.
The picture was *much* admired.
She is *much* changed from what she used to be.

But when a participle is used in a purely adjectival, and not a verbal, sense, then it is modified by *very*, in the same way that any other adjective would be.

She felt *very* tired.
We are *very* pleased to hear of your success.
I am *very* satisfied with my new house.

Other such participial adjectives are: annoyed, concerned, surprised, disappointed, interested, worried, bored, limited, shocked, swollen, heated (in the sense of *angry*), excited.

3 *Much*, not *very*, is used before *too*.

His speech was *much* too long.
He speaks *much* too quickly.

4 Neither *very* nor *much* can be used before a plain superlative, (We cannot say *This is much best* or *This is very best.*) but *much* can be used before a superlative preceded by *the*.

This way is *much the best.*
This is *much the best* way of doing it.

5 *Very* is never used to modify verbs. *Much* is fairly common *after* the verb in questions and in negative statements, and also in conditional clauses, which are half negative in that they envisage the possibility of the condition's non-fulfilment, as well as of its fulfilment.

Does the wound pain you much?
Have we damaged the car much?
I don't smoke much.
That child has not grown much during the past year.
If your tooth hurts you much, take one of these tablets.
A slight shower won't deter us, but if it rains much we shall have to abandon the outing.

The only verb in common use that takes *much* in positive statements is *prefer*. This is probably because it implies a comparison of two or more things, and so it falls in with the comparative degree of the adjectives and adverbs.

I much prefer this one to the other.
I much prefer cricket to football.

Notes

1. *Different*, though an adjective of the positive degree, implies a comparison. When used predicatively and preceded by *not* it generally takes *much*, but when *not* is absent it takes *very*.

She is *very different* from her sister.
This is *not much different* from the other.

When used attributively it always takes *very*.

> The village is now *a very different place* from what it was thirty years ago.

2. Certain adjectives which can be used only predicatively must take *much*: *afraid*, *alike*, *alone*, *obliged*.

> The twins were much alike.
> We are much obliged to you for your information.
> People who are much alone often become depressed.

3. In all its uses *much* may be preceded by *very* if it is desired to emphasise it: *very much alike*, *very much obliged*, *very much afraid*, *very much better*, *I don't smoke very much*.

EXERCISES

1 Supply *much* or *very* in the following sentences.

a He is ..... older than I thought.
b It is ..... cold today.
c She is ..... interested in history.
d You must speak ..... more clearly than that.
e I am ..... concerned about his health.
f It was ..... cruel of you to pull the cat's tail.
g I am feeling ..... better today.
h We are ..... obliged for the help you have given us.
i Do you come here ..... often?
j No, not ..... often but I should like to come ..... more often if I could.
k The box was ..... too heavy for me to lift.
l The children became ..... excited when they heard that their uncle was coming.
m That man is ..... esteemed for his kindness to the poor.
n Do you cycle ..... nowadays?
o This material is not ..... different from the other.
p He is reputed to be ..... rich.
q Her health is ..... improved compared with what it was a few months ago.
r We shall have to start ..... soon if we are to catch that train.
s You must do your work ..... more carefully than this.
t The exercise was ..... too difficult for the class to do.

2 Put *much* or *much the* in the blank spaces in the following sentences, in order to complete the sense.

a This way is ..... safer than the other.
b This way is ..... safest.
c Of all the methods we have tried this is ..... easiest.
d You couldn't have any method ..... easier than this.
e Of the three routes, we found that the one by which we came was ..... shortest.
f We stayed ..... later than we had intended.
g We arrived ..... sooner than we thought we should.
h He is a ..... better scholar than his brother.
i This is ..... warmest room in the house.
j He can speak English ..... more fluently than I can.

32. *Still* and *yet*

Foreign students of English often find difficulty with these two adverbs. The following are the chief points about them to remember.

Still denotes the continuance of some activity or situation from the past into the present.

> I still think that what I did was right. (i.e., I thought so previously and I have not altered my opinion.)
> It is still raining. (i.e., it was raining previously and it has not stopped.)
> Is your brother still at the universtiy? (i.e., I know he was there at one time. Has he left yet?)
> Tom has still got that book I lent him.

Yet presents the present situation in relation to the future.

> The rascal may have escaped me so far, but I'll catch him yet. (i.e., some time in the future)
> The train is not due yet. (i.e., it is due later)
> Has the doctor been yet? (i.e., or are we to expect him later?)

Don't cross the road yet; wait till the policeman gives the signal.
Is it three o'clock yet? (i.e., or is that hour still in the future?)
I have yet to meet a person who is satisfied with his job. (i.e., I have not met one up to now, so if I do meet one it will be in the future.)

Occasionally *still* and *yet* seem equally suitable:

We have *still* three miles to go.
We have three miles to go *yet*.

But though the two sentences may amount to the same, they do express slightly different views of the situation. The latter (with *yet*) thinks merely of the distance that lies ahead, without any reference to that which has already been traversed. The former (with *still*) thinks of it as a continuation of that which has been covered already.

In statements, *still* is usually placed before a simple tense form of a verb, except when it is a tense of the verb *to be;* then it usually follows the verb.

He is *still* very ill.
The wound is *still* painful.

If the verb is a compound tense form, *still* usually follows the first auxiliary. An exception occurs with the contracted negative forms *isn't*, *aren't*, *hasn't*, *haven't*, etc:

He is still not well enough to go to work.
My essay is still not finished.
He has still not done it.

But

He *still isn't* well enough to go to work.
My essay *still isn't* finished.
He *still hasn't* done it.

In questions *still* follows the subject.

Yet is usually placed at the end of the sentence or clause, though this is not an invariable rule, as will be seen from the last example in the list above. In negative sentences it often follows *not*.

He is *not yet* well enough to go to work.
Some of the guests have *not yet* arrived.
I hope to become a doctor, but I have *not yet* qualified.

EXERCISES

Supply *still* or *yet*, (whichever you think correct) in the following sentences.

1. When we set out at six o'clock in the morning it was ..... dark.
2. Are you ..... working for the same firm as when I saw you last?
3. Have you heard from your sister .....?
4. We can get to the station in about twenty minutes, and there's almost another hour before the train goes, so we needn't leave .....
5. I have not ..... made up my mind whether I shall accept his offer.
6. There were ten cigarettes in this packet, and I have smoked six, so there are ..... four left.
7. Does your daughter ..... go to school? Yes, she has not left ..... but she probably will be leaving next year.
8. He said he would write to us, but he has not written .....
9. I have oiled the hinge of the door, but it is ..... stiff.
10. I..... cannot give you the information, as I have not received it myself .....
11. When the doctor arrived the injured man was ..... breathing.
12. The weather forecast said that it would rain, but it is not raining .....

33. *Make* and *do*

Many foreign students of English find it difficult to decide when they should use *make* and when they should use *do* in order to translate a particular idea from their own language into English. As a rough guide the following principle may be laid down: if the general idea to be expressed is that of *create, manufacture, fashion, construct*, or *bring into being*, then *make* should be used. If the general idea is that of *act*, or *perform*, then *do* should be used.

Having laid down this general principle, we may now go into more detail.

1 The chief meanings of *make* are as follows:

(*a*) Create, fashion or produce (The object is a noun.)

God made the world.
Cutlery is made in Sheffield.
Bread is made from flour.
That box is made of wood.
You have made a mistake in that exercise.
Do not make so much noise.

(*b*) Prove to be, on account of some quality or talent one possesses (The object is again a noun.)

That young fellow would make a good teacher.
He will never make a scholar.
I should make a bad sailor, as I am always ill if the sea is rough.
That story would make a good subject for a novel.

(*c*) Cause (Here *make* is followed by an accusative and an infinitive without *to*.)

The sun makes the plants grow.
The noise made us start.
The clown's antics made the children laugh.

(*d*) Cause to be. (Here *make* is followed by an accusative and an adjective used predicatively to refer to the accusative.)

The poisonous berries made him ill.
The hot sun made us sleepy.

(*e*) Compel. (Here the construction is the same as that in (*c*). *Make* is followed by an accusative and an infinitive without *to*.)

The teacher made the pupil repeat the work.
The robber made the travellers give him their money.

Note, however, that though the infinitive without *to* is used after the active voice of *make*, after the passive voice *to* must be used.

The travellers were made *to give* their money to the robber.
The pupil was made *to repeat* his work.

2 The following are the chief meanings of *do:*
(*a*) Act

Do as I tell you.
He has always been allowed to do as he wishes.
You did quite right, to refuse to lend him the money.

(*b*) Perform, or carry out

He did the task without complaining.
I cannot do this exercise.
We were fascinated by the way the conjuror did his tricks.
One cannot do impossibilities.

(*c*) Perform some activity relating to the object of the verb, which is unspecified but is implied from the context

He employed a man to do the garden. (i.e., attend to)
She spent ten minutes doing her hair. (i.e., brushing, combing and making tidy)
Would you like me to do you some bacon for your breakfast? (i.e., cook)

Here are some typical expressions in which the two verbs are used.

Make: make a garment, make an object, article, make some product, make a noise, make a mistake, make a decision, make a suggestion, make a journey, make a fuss, make up one's mind, make up a story, a poem, make fun of, make friends, make love, make out (meaning ' pretend ').

Do: do some work, do a task, do one's duty, do one's homework, do one's best. Note also the greeting or salutation, *How do you do*? meaning ' How are you getting on?'

The following tables give examples of misuses of *make* and *do* that are sometimes found in the speech or writing of foreign students of English. The wrong construction is given in the first column, the correct one in the second.

Incorrect uses of *Make*	Correct Version
He made me an injury.	He did me an injury.
I have made my examination.	I have taken my examination.
We made a short walk.	We went for a short walk. We took a short walk.
I make a bath each morning.	I have a bath each morning. I take a bath each morning.
I have made my breakfast.	I have had my breakfast.
Have you made your breakfast?	Have you had your breakfast?
She is making her prayers.	She is saying her prayers.

Incorrect uses of *Do*	Correct Version
You have done a mistake.	You have made a mistake.
The tailor did me a suit.	The tailor made me a suit.
He did a theft.	He committed a theft.
I did him a blow in the chest.	I gave him a blow in the chest.
He did me some valuable help.	He gave me some valuable help.

EXERCISES

1 Insert in the following sentences some part of the verb *do* or *make* (whichever you think correct).

a The sudden pain ..... him cry out.
b I must get the tailor to ..... me a new suit.
c We have now ..... all the work that was set for us.
d The teacher asked the class to ..... the exercise in their note books.
e That person once ..... me a great kindness.
f This heavy rain will ..... the ground very wet.
g You have ..... three mistakes in one sentence.
h If you inherited a fortune, what would you ..... with it?
i He is very interested in ...... model aeroplanes.
j Many motor-cars are ..... in Coventry.
k She ..... a great effort to ..... the work.
l Nothing will persuade me to ..... what I know to be wrong.
m We all admire a person who ..... a brave deed.
n Who is ..... that noise?
o Could you please ..... me a favour?

p You can't trust that man; he says one thing and then ..... something else.
q You cannot ..... silk purses out of sows' ears. (An English proverb)
r You ought to ..... those children behave better.
s This poor light ..... it very difficult for us to read.
t He always ..... what he promises.
u Take this medicine; it will ..... you good.
v She ..... the child a dress out of the piece of silk I gave her.
w A boy scout is supposed to ..... at least one good turn each day.
x John is still ..... his homework.
y I will bring the parcel next time I come; I do not want to ..... a special journey to deliver it.

2 Point out the difference of meaning between the sentences in each of the following pairs.
(*a*) Those children make a lot of work for me.
(*b*) Those children do a lot of work for me.

(*a*) She made a good meal.
(*b*) She had a good meal.

(*a*) She is always making complaints.
(*b*) She is always having complaints.

34. The verb *have*

In American English *have* presents no difficulties, since it is treated, in all its meanings, as a regular verb. An American will say:

I don't have any money,

and will ask:

Do you have any cigarettes to spare?

This is beginning to appear in British English also, but traditional British usage, which in Britain is still considered strictly correct, makes a distinction between *have* when it denotes possession or some idea akin to it, and *have* when it expresses other meanings. Only in the latter case does it follow the regular pattern, using the *do* forms for the negative and the interrogative.

When the meaning of *have* is ' possess ' (or when it expresses some idea closely connected with that of possession), in the present tense, the negative and the interrogative forms are *have not* (*haven't*) and *have + subject*? respectively if the reference is to a specific occasion; the forms with *do* are reserved for what is general, recurrent, or habitual.

> I haven't any money. (not *I don't have any money*, if the reference is to the present moment.)
> Have you any brothers or sisters? (not *do you have*?)

But

> I don't have any pocket money. (i.e., As a general rule I do not receive any.)
> Do you have any pocket money? (i.e., Do you generally receive any?)

Note also the following pairs.

> Have you indigestion? (now)
> Do you have indigestion? (not necessarily now, but do you suffer from it as a general rule?)
>
> Have you much homework to do? (now)
> Do you have much homework to do? (generally)
>
> I haven't a secretary. (The position at the moment, either because she has left or because I never have one.)
> I don't have a secretary. (This makes it clear that the reference is to the general position, and not merely the position at the moment.)

In the past tense the distinction is not so definite or so important. The tendency with most British speakers is perhaps still to prefer the plain form (without *do*) for the specific occasion, but the form with *do* is also frequently heard.

> I hadn't enough money to pay the bill.
> I didn't have enough money to pay the bill.
> Had you any difficulty in finding the house?
> Did you have any difficulty in finding the house?

The plain form is certainly the more idiomatic of the two:

(*a*) When the fact or situation in question is looked at from the point of view of a particular moment in the past, not from that of the moment of speaking.

> When I got to the counter I found that *I hadn't* enough money to pay the bill. (not *didn't have enough money*)

(*b*) When it occurs in a negative indirect statement or question which, for the direct form, would use *haven't* or *haven't* +*subject*.

> He said that he *hadn't* time to see me. (not *didn't have time*)

What he would actually say in the direct form would be, *I haven't time to see you.*

> I asked him whether he *hadn't* enough money to pay the bill. (not *didn't have enough money*)

The direct question would be, *Haven't you enough money to pay the bill?*

Notes

1. Positive indirect questions never use the form with *do*, no matter whether the corresponding direct question would use it or not. This is because indirect questions follow the same syntactic pattern as statements, and positive statements do not use *do*. (*I went*—positive statement: *Did you go?*—direct question: *I asked him whether he went*—indirect question.) So the two questions given above, *Have you indigestion?* and *Do you have indigestion?* despite their difference of meaning, would both be rendered in the indirect form, *I inquired whether he had indigestion.*

2. Auxiliary *have* never uses the *do* form.

> Have you read his latest novel? (not *do you have read?*)
> I have not read his latest novel. (not *I do not have read*)

EXERCISES

1 Write the negative forms of the following sentences.

a I have a headache today.
b That boy has a cap on.
c He has a lot of friends.

d We had a very enjoyable holiday.
e They have breakfast at eight o'clock every morning.
f I have indigestion if I eat rich food.
g My sister has a diamond necklace.
h I always have a rest after my lunch.
i The teacher has a great deal of patience.
j That girl has a book in her hand.
k The cyclist had a very bad accident.
l We have a lot of work to do today.
m I have something to tell you. (Change *something* to *anything* in the negative version of the sentence.)
n We had a game of football yesterday.
o We always have a cup of tea in the middle of the afternoon.
p I have read Shakespeare's tragedy, *Hamlet*.
q That pupil has a good knowledge of English.
r Mrs Smith has several children. (Change *several* to *any* in the negative version.)
s She often has a cold.
t I have enough money to pay the bill for both of us.

2 Frame the question to which each of the sentences given in Exercise **1** might be the answer. See that you use the verb *have* in your question, and that you use the right form of it.

3 Rewrite the following sentences so as to bring out the same meaning, but using a negative form of *have* followed by *any*, instead of the positive form followed by *no*, e.g. *I have no money—I haven't any money. Have you no work to do?—Haven't you any work to do?* You will sometimes need to use the plain form of *have*, and sometimes the form with *do*.

a I had no breakfast this morning.
b Mrs Jones has no children.
c The starving family had no food to eat.
d I have no idea where he is.
e An orphan is a child who has no parents.
f I have no patience with a person who acts so foolishly.
g As a rule she has no sugar in her tea.
h We have no intention of selling the house.
i I usually have no trouble to get my car to start.
j You have no right to that piece of land.

k They have no experience of this kind of work.
l Mr Brown is a vegetarian, so he has no meat for his meals.
m When Mrs Brown got to the butcher's shop, it was closed, so the Browns have no meat for their dinner.
n Have you no medicine you can take for that cough?
o I have no engagement on Tuesday evening.

35. *Shall* and *will*

In British English the future tense of a verb has the auxiliary *shall* in the first person, both singular and plural, and *will* in the other two persons[1]. When *will* is used in the first person it denotes some degree of volition on the part of the subject: that is, it expresses his desire, willingness, intention or determination.

Accordingly, if you are following British usage:

1 Use *shall*, not *will*, in the first person when the fact stated is such that one's own will or desire can play no part in it.

> I *shall* be eighteen on my next birthday. (not *I will be*)
> If we go by the 10.30 train, when *shall* we arrive at our destination? (not *will we*)
> I do not know whether I *shall* be able to come. (not *will be able*)

2 If you are making an offer or a promise, or expressing your determination or intention, use *will* for the first person.

> I *will* carry that parcel for you. (I am willing to: an offer)
> We *will* meet you at ten o'clock. (A promise)
> I *will* never have that person in my house again. (Intention or determination.)

[1] American English uses *will* for all persons. This is also beginning to appear in the English of Great Britain, but for the first person it is not yet accepted.

3 The same auxiliaries are used in questions.

When *shall* we know the result of the examination? (Future)
Shall I get to London by midday if I go by this train? (Future)
When *will you* be sixteen? (Future)
Will you carry this parcel for me, please? (A request. Literally, *Are you willing to?*)

As a speaker does not usually inquire of others about his own willingness to do something, *will* is not normally used in first person questions, except:

(*a*) As an echo of a previous request in which *will you?* was used.

Will I? Of course I will.

(*b*) As a tag question attached to a statement that uses *won't.*

We won't allow it, will we?

This is confined almost exclusively to the plural, where the speaker puts the question to the others comprised in *we*, and asks for their confirmation of his statement.

There is a conjugation that uses *shall* for all persons. In statements it expresses the will, determination or intention, not of the subject, but of the speaker regarding the subject.

You shall have whatever you need.
You shall not go short of money.
My son shall have the best education possible.

Here the speaker is stating what he has determined or decided regarding *you* and *my son.*

In questions it asks the will or desire of the person addressed regarding the subject.

Shall I close the window? (i.e., *Would you like me to close the window?*)
Shall we go for a walk? (i.e., *Do you agree?* or *Would you like to?*)
Shall John bring the parcel when he calls next Friday? (i.e., *Do you wish him to?*)

So if you wish to state what your decision or determination is regarding some other person or thing, use *shall* for the second and third persons. If you wish to ask whether another person desires you or someone else to do something, use *shall* for the first and third persons.

Notes

1. If a suggestion made by the use of *we will* has a tag asking for confirmation, the tag is *shall we?*, not *will we?*

> We'll stop (i.e., we will stop) and have a cup of tea now, shall we?

The speaker first makes the suggestion on behalf of the whole group, and then asks whether it is acceptable to the others.

2. When put into the past, *will* becomes *would*, and *shall* becomes *should;* but remember that when direct speech is changed to indirect, and a first person has to be changed to a third person, *I/we shall* (if it expresses the future tense) becomes *he/they would* (not *should*).

Direct ' I *shall* be sixteen on my next birthday,' he said.
Indirect He said that he *would* be sixteen on his next birthday.
Direct When *shall* we know the result of the examination?
Indirect They asked when they *would* know the result of the examination.

3. In spoken English the following contracted forms are commonly used:

Shall and *Will* are contracted to *'ll* (I'll, you'll, he'll, she'll, we'll, they'll) in the future simple.
Shall has no contracted form when indicating a promise:
You shall have your money back; I promise you.
Will not is contracted to *won't.*
Shall not is contracted to *shan't.*
Would is contracted to *'d.* (He would like—He'd like)
Should is contracted to *'d.* (I should like—I'd like.)
Would not is contracted to *wouldn't.*
Should not is contracted to *shouldn't.*

EXERCISES

1 Fill in the blank spaces in the following sentences with *will* or *shall* in order to complete the future tense.

a We ..... all die one day.
b I am now twenty-five, so in one year's time I ..... be twenty-six.
c ..... you be thirty or thirty-one on your next birthday?
d I think we ..... get some rain before the day is out.
e When ..... the goods arrive?
f When ..... we know who has won the competition?
g I ..... have only five pounds left when I have paid all the bills I owe.
h ..... Uncle John be at the party?
i ..... we see him there?
j It ..... be ten o'clock by the time we get home.
k If we do not hurry the shops ..... be shut.
l I ..... be sorry to leave such a pleasant place as this.

2 Express the meaning of the following sentences by using *shall* or *will*, e.g. *When is your sixteenth birthday?—When will you be sixteen?*

N.B. You may sometimes have to replace a statement by a question.

a I should like you to close the window.
b Do you think it is likely to rain?
c My eighteenth birthday is on June 5th.
d Do you wish me to post that letter?
e I promise you not to do it again.
f We have decided not to go.
g If you do not work harder you are certain to fail.
h I think I am unlikely to live to be a hundred.
i I am not going to allow anything to stop me doing what I think right.
j That cat is certain to scratch you if you tease it.
k I suggest that we have a game of tennis.
l The years that are past we are certain not to see again.
m The Prime Minister is to address the conference on Tuesday.
n When is this train likely to arrive in London?

o Would you like me to write to them, or do you intend to? (Two alterations are needed here, one in each clause.)
p Do you wish Tom to bring any food with him?
q When is the book likely to be published?
r How are we going to let them know where to find us?
s Please fill in the enclosed form.
t Let's go and get a cup of coffee. Do you agree to that? (Express as one sentence.)

36. *Used to* (verb) and *to be used to*

A. USED TO

In the sentence *People used to think that the earth was flat*, the word *used* is the past tense of a verb; it cannot, therefore, be preceded by an auxiliary. A mistake sometimes made by foreign students of English is to say:

People *were* used to think that the earth was flat.

This is incorrect, and care should be taken to avoid it. Note also that *used*, in this construction, is always followed by an infinitive, the two going together to make up a special kind of past tense of the infinitive. There are two chief uses of it.

1 To state what was generally, always or repeatedly the case in the past—not merely what happened on one occasion. This is illustrated in the example given above. Here are some other examples.

If the weather was fine, I used to walk home from work each evening.
A large house used to stand on this spot.
When I was a boy we used to go to school on Saturday morning.

2 To contrast the past with the present.

I live in Manchester now, but I used to live at Brighton.
I used to read quite a lot of detective stories, but recently I have lost interest in them.

The negative of *used to* is generally expressed by *used not to.*

I used not to smoke; I took it up about three years ago.

But *didn't use to* is also found; and this is nearly always used in questions.

I think I know that person. Didn't he use to keep a shop in this town?

B. TO BE USED TO

Young children will often object to eating food that they are not used to.

Here *used* is an adjective, meaning 'accustomed', and *to* a preposition. It must therefore be preceded by a tense of the verb *be, get* or *become* (be used to, get used to, become used to) or by a verb of similar meaning. The only verbal form that can follow it is the gerund; otherwise it is followed by a noun or pronoun. It can never be followed by an infinitive.

Followed by a noun or pronoun

The dog was not used to strangers.
You will not find the climate so oppressive when you get used to it.

Followed by a gerund

I am not used to walking long distances. (not *I am not used to walk long distances.*)
They soon got used to living in the country. (not *got used to live in the country.*)

When *used to* is used in this sense there is no negative of it. It may be used in negative sentences, but the negative word belongs to the verb, not to the adjective *used.* An example will be found in the first sentence given above. Here are two others.

He *had not been used* to such a hot climate.
I *cannot get used* to drinking tea without any sugar in it.

EXERCISES

1 Insert *used* followed by an infinitive, or *used to* followed by a gerund, in the blank spaces in the following sentences. The verb you should use is given in brackets at the end of each sentence.

a A very well-known person ..... in this house. (live)
b That car ..... to a friend of mine. (belong)
c He was not ..... so hard. (work)
d I ..... that if you drank too much tea you would get drunk. (think)
e I always .....tired when I lived in that place. (feel)
f At first she was very shy, as she had not been ..... people. (meet)
g Where I lived as a boy we never ..... snow in winter. (have)
h My father ..... that health was better than money. (say)
i The spot where a prosperous town now stands, at one time ..... a barren waste. (be)
j A hundred years ago most people ..... much longer hours than they do now. (work)
k I am not ..... such long hours. (work)
l He was not ..... at such an unearthly hour. (get up)

2 Express the sense of the following sentences by using *used to.*

a At one time I was a teacher, but now I am a business man.
b Our school was formerly a large private house.
c In past times the climate was much warmer than it is now.
d There was once a bridge across the river at this point.
e For some time after I left home I wrote to my mother every week.
f At one time people believed that a mad person was possessed of a devil.
g In my earlier life I imagined that I should be perfectly happy if I had plenty of money.
h Outbreaks of plague are not so frequent as they were at one time.
i At one time it was thought that there were lands where giants existed.
j When we were children our mother would read us a story each night before we went to bed.

3 Write five sentences of your own using *used* as a verb followed by an infinitive, and five using *used* as an adjective followed by *to*.

37. *So that* and *so as*

Both these expressions show purpose, but *so that* introduces a clause, whereas *so as* introduces an infinitive or an infinitive construction.

> They arrived early, *so that* they might get a good seat.
> (not *so as they might get a good seat*)
> They arrived early *so as* to get a good seat.
> (not *so that to get a good seat.*)

EXERCISES

Complete the following sentences by inserting *so as* or *so that* in the blank spaces.

a He put some oil on the hinge, ... it should not squeak.
b They started in good time ..... they should not be late.
c We went by a side street ..... to avoid the crowds.
d She stepped very quietly across the room, ... she should not wake the baby.
e He wiped his shoes carefully, ... not to bring any dirt into the house.
f He took his brother with him ..... to have a companion on the journey.
g They hid behind a wall, ... no-one would see them.
h I stayed up late that night ..... I might finish the book.
i Carry the jar carefully, ... you do not spill any of the contents.
j She added the figures up twice, ... to make sure the total was correct.
k They destroyed all the papers, ... no-one should know what information they contained.

l ..... to escape notice, he slipped out by a back door.
m They packed the goods securely, ... they should not get damaged.
n The two boys took plenty of food with them, ... they should not be hungry.
o He took a revolver with him, ... to defend himself in case of attack.

38. Errors in the use of individual words

It would be impossible to give here a full list of words in the use of which foreign students of English are apt to make errors, but the following are some of the commoner of them. In each case the error is pointed out and the correct version is given. The list is arranged alphabetically.

ABROAD *Abroad* is an adverb, not a noun.

I should like to travel abroad. (not *in the abroad*)

Abroad is never preceded by an article, and not usually by a preposition, but *from abroad* is correct in sentences like the following:

We are always pleased to welcome visitors from abroad.

ADMIRE *Admire* is a transitive verb, and therefore takes a direct object.

Everyone admired his courage. (not *admired at his courage*)

ALSO *Also* is used only in positive sentences. In negative sentences it is replaced by *neither* or by *nor.*

Positive He is clever and also industrious.
Negative He is not clever, neither is he industrious (or *nor is he industrious*, but not *nor also is he industrious.*)

ATTENTION

Pay attention to what I am saying. (not *give attention*)
Similarly: Pay attention to your work.

He paid no attention to the instructions that were given him.

But if *attention* is preceded by a possessive adjective, then *give* must be used.

Give your attention to your work.
I will give the matter my attention.
Give me your attention for a few moments.

BORROW See LEND
BRIEFLY See SHORTLY
BRING/FETCH *Bring* means 'convey from some distant point to the speaker, or to some place or person that is mentioned.'

Bring me your book.
Did you bring your homework to school?

Fetch means 'go and get (something), and then bring it here'.

Will you please fetch me my hat and coat?
Mother has gone to fetch Johnny from school.

The activity of bringing starts from the distant point, that of fetching from the point at which the speaker is stationed (or sometimes from that where the person addressed is stationed, if it is not near the thing that is to be conveyed). Thus a teacher says to a pupil at the back of the class, *Bring me your book*. But if he has called the pupil out to the front, and then sends him back for the book, he will say *Fetch me your book*.

CELEBRATE : CONGRATULATE We *congratulate* a person on something he has done or achieved, but we celebrate the achievement or the occasion when we hold some function in honour of it.

We congratulated him on winning a scholarship. (not *celebrated*)
To *celebrate* his winning a scholarship, the school was given a half-holiday.

COWARD : COWARDLY *Coward* is a noun. The adjective from it is *cowardly*.

He is a coward.
He is a cowardly person. (not *a coward person*)
He is very cowardly (not *very coward*)
That was a cowardly thing to do. (not *a coward thing*)

DAMAGE *Damage* is a singular noun. In its normal sense of *destruction* or *injury* it is not used in the plural.

The explosion caused much damage. (not *many damages*)
Was there much damage done? (not *many damages*)

But there is a word *damages* with the meaning of ' a sum of money awarded to a person by a court of law as compensation for any loss or injury he may have suffered '.

DEAL We deal cards (distribute them amongst the players), and deal a blow to someone; but deal *with* a matter, a subject, a question or a problem.

I will deal *with* that question in the next lesson. (not *I will deal that question*)
You will find the matter *dealt with* on page six of your text book.

We may also *deal with* a person (meaning 'to act towards' or ' treat ')

The magistrates dealt with the offender very leniently.

A tradesman deals *in* the goods he sells.

An uncle of mine deals in second-hand books.

DENY : REFUSE *Refuse* means ' decline to take something that is offered ' or ' to do something that one is asked to do '.

He refused the money (not *He denied the money*)
The thief refused to disclose where he had hidden the stolen property. (not *The thief denied to disclose*)

Deny means (*a*) assert that something is not true, (*b*) withhold (something) from a person.

The prisoner denied the charge.
He denied that he had stolen the goods.
Her parents deny her nothing she asks for.

DISCUSS *Discuss* is a transitive verb, and therefore takes a direct object.

We will discuss that matter later. (not *discuss about that matter*)
They spent over an hour discussing their plans.

EXPLAIN This verb does not take an indirect object in the dative case. The person to whom the explanation is given must be indicated by the preposition *to*.

The speaker explained his proposals *to the committee.*
He explained *to us* why it was necessary to take such great care.

not { The speaker explained the committee his proposals.
He explained us why it was necessary to take such great care. }

FETCH See BRING

FUN See JOKE

FURNITURE: FURNISHINGS *Furniture* includes tables, chairs, wardrobes, bedsteads, couches and cabinets, but not such things as carpets, rugs and curtains. These latter are known as *furnishings.*

Furnishings is a plural. *Furniture* is a collective singular (cf. luggage, cutlery, crockery). There is no plural form of it.

There is too much furniture in the room. (not *too many furnitures*)
We have sold some of our furniture. (not *furnitures*)

An individual item is *a piece of furniture.*

The contents of the room consisted of a carpet and a few pieces of furniture. (not *a few furnitures*)

HIGH : TALL *Tall*, not *high*, is used to describe the stature of a person.

That man is very tall. (not *high*)

It is also used of things such as trees, stems of flowers, flagstaffs, chimney stacks and spires, which tower to a great height. *High* refers to distance from the ground or the floor: e.g. a high shelf, a high window, a high roof. When we speak of a *tall* chimney stack we are referring to its appearance; when we speak of a *high* chimney stack we are referring merely to the distance from the ground to the top of it.

HOPE : WISH *Wish* merely expresses a desire, *hope* a desire which one is anxious to see fulfilled, or which one expects will be fulfilled.

I hope you will pass your examination. (not *wish*)
We hope to finish the work by the end of the week.

I wish to see Mr Brown this afternoon means merely that I desire to see him. *I hope to see Mr Brown this afternoon* means that I desire to see him, and expect that I shall.

Hope can be applied only to something that has not yet happened, whereas *wish* can be used of something that we should like to have been otherwise than it was.

> I hope to succeed. (I have not succeeded yet.)
> I wish I had succeeded. (This implies that I did not succeed.)

JOKE : FUN We have *fun* (i.e., enjoy ourselves) and make *fun* of a person (i.e., ridicule him), but we *make a joke* (i.e., say something humorous) or *play a joke* on someone (i.e., play an amusing trick on him).

> The comedian made many good jokes. (not *funs*)
> The small boy played a joke on his father. (not *a fun*)

I only said it in fun and *I only said it in joke* mean more or less the same (though the former is more frequently used). We say *I only did it for a joke*, but not *I only did it for a fun.*

Fun can never take the indefinite article, but a definite article is quite common.

> The children were enjoying the fun.

KNOW To indicate that a person knows the way or the method of doing something, *know* cannot be followed merely by the infinitive; the infinitive must be preceded by *how*. (See p. 120)

> I don't know *how* to do it. (not *I don't know to do it.*)
> Do you know *how* to make ice-cream? (not *Do you know to make ice-cream?*)

LAY : LIE *Lay* (past tense *laid*) is transitive, and must therefore have an object. *Lie* (past tense *lay*) is intransitive, and has no object.

> If you are tired, go and lie down. (not *lay down*)
> The sick person lay on the bed. (not *laid on the bed*)
> Lay the injured person on this rug. (not *lie*)

LEARN See TEACH

LEND : BORROW The person to whom a thing belongs *lends* it to someone else (i.e., allows him the use of it temporarily);

the person to whom it is lent *borrows* it from its owner; i.e. has the use of it temporarily.

May I *borrow* your English dictionary? (not *lend*)
Will you *lend* me your English dictionary?

LIE See LAY

LOAN This word is a noun (*He asked me for a loan of five pounds*). In recent years there has been a tendency to use it also as a verb, but it is better not so used, since *lend* is already available for this purpose.

He asked me to *lend* him five pounds. (not *to loan him five pounds*)

LUGGAGE This is a collective noun, and takes a singular verb. There is no plural form of it, since it is plural in sense already.

Where is your luggage? (not *Where are your luggages?*)
Have you much luggage? (not *Have you many luggages?*)
His luggage was very heavy. (not *His luggages were .....*)

MEANS When *means*=method, it is singular; when it has the sense of 'resources' it is plural.

By *this means* we shall save much time and money. (not *by these means*)
My bicycle is my *one means* of getting to work.
His means *are* small. (i.e., He has not much money)

Note the phrase *by means of* (not *by the means of*).
The boat was propelled by means of oars.

MIND (Noun) We *make up* our mind to do something (not *set up* our mind).

He made up his mind to retire when he reached the age of sixty.
I cannot make up my mind whether to go or not.

NO SOONER No sooner should be followed by *than*, not by *when*.

No sooner had the cricket match started, than it began to rain. (not *when it began to rain*)

Sooner is a comparative degree of the adverb *soon*, and comparatives are followed by *than*.

OBEY This verb is transitive, and therefore takes a direct object. It is not followed by *to*.

Children should obey their parents. (not *to their parents*)
Good citizens obey the law. (not *to the law*)

PASSED : PAST Write *passed* only when the word is a verb; in all other cases write *past*.

They *passed* the time by doing crossword puzzles.
It was half *past* ten when they *passed* the Town Hall.
The time *has passed* very quickly.
Someone has just gone *past*. (Adverb)
They walked *past* the window. (Preposition)
She is always talking about *past* times. (Adjective)
The age of miracles is *past*. (Adjective used predicatively)
We cannot live in the *past*. (Noun)
The *past* tense of the verb ' to eat ' is ' ate '. (adjective)

PREVENT The verb *prevent* is never followed by an accusative +infinitive. It is incorrect to say :

The darkness prevented us to see the obstruction.

The correct constructions are either.

The darkness prevented *our seeing* the obstruction.

or

The darkness prevented *us from seeing* the obstruction.

PUT : KEEP *Put* denotes a momentary action, which is completed when the thing in question is left in the place where we ' put ' it.

He *put* the letter in his pocket.
Put your book on the desk.

Keep denotes

(*a*) The continuance of an activity, or continuance in a certain state or position.

Put your hands on your head and *keep* them there.
Keep turning the handle till I tell you to stop.

(*b*) Place (a thing) somewhere permanently.

The miser *kept* his money in an old oak chest.
Where do you *keep* the biscuits?

(*c*) Retain possession of.

You may *keep* the book until you have read it.
The fact that you find a thing does not entitle you to *keep* it.

(*d*) Maintain in food and clothing.

He earns scarcely enough to *keep* himself.
While he was at the university he *was kept* by his father.

REFUSE See DENY

REMEMBER: REMIND We ourselves *remember* something (i.e., call it back to mind); we *remind* another person of something we think he may have forgotten.

I remember meeting your cousin about two years ago.
His face is familiar to me, but I cannot *remember* his name.
You must *remind* me to post these letters. (not *you must remember me*)
I *reminded* him of his promise. (not *remembered him*)

A thing or a sight may also *remind* us of something, and one person may remind us of another: i.e., bring him to our mind because of a resemblance.

This place reminds me of a small village I once visited in southern England.
That young fellow over there reminds me of your brother Joe.

ROB: STEAL The things taken by a thief are *stolen*, and the thief *steals* them; the person or the place they are taken from is *robbed*, and the thief *robs* them of the things.

The thief *stole* some valuable rings. (not *robbed*)
The car in which they escaped was *stolen*. (not *robbed*)
I have been *robbed* of all my wealth.
They planned *to rob* a bank.
The dishonest young man even *robbed* his father.

Steal can also be used intransitively (Thou shalt not steal). Sometimes the person or place from whom or from which the goods are stolen is named after the verb.

He was fined for stealing *from a shop*.
He was suspected of stealing *from his employer*.

SCARCELY Scarcely must be followed by *when*, not *than*.

He had scarcely set foot on the road *when* he was knocked down by a car. (not *than*) See also NO SOONER.

SELDOM Do not use *seldomly*. There is no such word. *Seldom* is already an adverb, and so needs no adverbial suffix.

He *seldom* comes to see me. (not *seldomly*)
I go there very *seldom* (not *seldomly*)

SELL: BUY When a person parts with something in exchange for money, he *sells* it; when he acquires it by paying for it he *buys* it.

SHORTLY: BRIEFLY *Shortly* is an adverb of time, and means 'very soon'. *Briefly* is an adverb of manner, and means 'in a few words' or 'simply'.

They will be here *shortly* (i.e., very soon)
I have only time to tell you very *briefly* what he said. (i.e., in a few words)
I will tell you the story *shortly*. (i.e., not now, but very soon)
I will tell you the story *briefly*. (i.e., in a few words, without going into detail)

SHUT Foreign students of English sometimes use this verb wrongly. We can only *shut* something that is open (a door, a window, one's eyes).

It is incorrect to say:

Shut the tap.
Shut the electric light.

The correct versions are:

Turn off the tap.
Turn off (of *switch off*) the light.

STEAL See ROB
TALL See HIGH

TEACH: LEARN *Teach* means 'instruct' or 'give out knowledge'; *learn* means 'gain knowledge (or skill)'. The pupil or the student learns; the person who instructs him teaches.

Mr Johnson *teaches* us mathematics. (Not *learns us mathematics.*)
I am *learning* mathematics from Mr Johnson.

Experience may also *teach* us, or we may *learn* from experience.

TELL: SAY *Say* merely means to express in words, usually in speech, but it may also be in writing or in print (What does that notice say?). Although anything that is written, printed, or spoken is usually intended for others, the verb *say* itself does not mean to communicate only to other people. *Tell* means to convey information or an instruction by means of words.

Can you hear what he is *saying*?
He would not *tell* us where he had been. (not *say us*)
You should not *tell* lies. (not *say lies*)
I am quite sure she is *telling* the truth. (not *saying the truth*)
The porter *told* them that the train had left five minutes ago. (not *said them*)
The teacher told the class to open their books to page 53. (not *said the class*)

Tell, as stated above, can be used only for giving information or giving an instruction. *Say* is a more general term, and can be used for: statements, instructions, commands, questions, exclamations and invitations.

'Will you walk into my parlour?' *said* the spider to the fly.

In indirect speech, however, only statements can depend upon *say*. For questions, commands, instructions and invitations *tell*, *ask* or *inquire* must be used, whichever is appropriate, even if *say* is used in the direct form.

'I didn't expect you to arrive so early,' she said.
She said that she did not expect us to arrive so early.

But:

'How long do you intend to stay?' she said.
She *asked* us how long we intended to stay. (not *said us*)
'Don't get alarmed,' he said.
He *told* us not to get alarmed. (not *he said us*)
'Take a seat, please', said the young lady.
The young lady *asked* us to take a seat (or *told us to take a seat*).

TOO When *too* means 'also' or 'in addition', it can be used only in positive sentences. In negative sentences it is replaced by *neither*, or by *not.....either*.

She lost her handbag and her purse, too.
I said he would fail, and he did, too.
She has not found her handbag, or her purse, either.
I said he would not succeed, and he didn't, either. (or *neither did he*)

USED TO See p. 175

WAIT This verb, when used alone (i.e., without a preposition attached to it), is intransitive.

We waited half an hour.
We shall not wait after six o'clock.

Only when it is followed by *for* can it have an object.

I will wait *for* you at the bus stop. (not *I will wait you*)
Who are you waiting *for*? (not *Who are you waiting*?)

WIN : BEAT We *win* a game, a contest, a war, a battle or a prize. We *beat* an opponent.

We *won* the football match by three goals to nil.
We *beat* our opponents by three goals to nil. (not *we won our opponents*)
Jack *beat* me at marbles. (not *Jack won me*)
Tom *beat* all the other competitors, and so *won* the prize.

WISH: See HOPE

WITH : BY *By* denotes the agent (i.e., the doer) of some action; *with* denotes the instrument used.

The conspirators were pardoned *by* the king.
The windows were shattered *by* the explosion.

He was knocked down *by* a car (not *with a car*)
He hit me *with* a stick. (not *by a stick*)

We come, go or travel *by* bus, train, tram, taxi, aeroplane, car or bicycle, but *on* foot (not *by foot*).

By, however, is used only when the name of the vehicle is used in a general sense, to denote the *means* of transport. Note, incidentally, that in this sense it is not preceded by an article.

We shall go by train. (not' by *a* train ' or ' by *the* train ')

If a particular or individual vehicle is referred to, then *by* cannot be used.

We came *by* car.	I come to school *by* bicycle.
We came *in* our car.	I come to school *on* my bicycle.
They arrived *by* taxi.	He made the journey *by* aeroplane. (or *by air*)
They arrived *in* a taxi.	He made the journey *in* his own aeroplane.

EXERCISES

A Fill in the blank spaces in the following sentences by inserting whichever of the alternatives given at the end you think is the correct one.

1. It needed several porters to carry all his ..... (luggages, luggage)
2. You had better ..... some food with you, in case you get hungry. (bring, fetch)
3. This is not my own bicycle; I have ..... it from a friend. (lent, borrowed)
4. He had lived ..... for a good many years. (abroad, in the abroad)
5. I am going to ..... down for half an hour. (lie, lay)
6. Could you ..... me your pencil, please? (borrow, lend)
7. That young fellow is never serious; he is always making ..... (funs, jokes)
8. His uncle sells second-hand ..... (furnitures, furniture)
9. I ..... the weather would improve. (wish, hope)
10. That girl is very ..... for her age. (tall, high)

11. You must ..... the instructions of the teacher. (obey, obey to)
12. In the table-tennis tournament the girls ..... the boys. (won, beat)
13. The manager asked his secretary to .... him to telephone his bank at 2.30. (remember, remind)
14. The thief broke into the safe and ..... all the money. (robbed, stole)
15. We ..... see such a sight as this. (seldom, seldomly)
16. She ..... to say where she had bought the ring. (denied, refused)
17. He had scarcely recovered from one illness ...... he had another. (than, when)
18. The facts of the case are ..... as follows. (shortly, briefly)
19. Miss Mercer ..... us English. (teaches, learns)
20. She would not ..... how old she was. (say, tell)
21. She would not ..... us how old she was. (say, tell)
22. We shall not ..... any late-comers. (wait, wait for)
23. Move on, please; you cannot ..... here. (wait, wait for)
24. That student is not very clever, and he is not very fond of work, ... (too, either)
25. In my younger days I ..... do a good deal of walking. (used to, was used to).
26. Our dog has been run over and killed ..... a car. (with, by)
27. This letter was written ..... a pen. (with, by)
28. Uncle Tom is a very jolly person; he is full of ..... (fun, joke)
29. No sooner had we set out ..... a thunder storm occurred. (when, than)
30. Have you yet ...... up your mind where you will go for your holidays? (set, made)
31. Do you ..... to repair a puncture? (know, know how)
32. We are now at the top of the ..... mountain in the country. (tallest, highest)
33. I ..... I had taken your advice. (hope, wish)
34. May I ..... my coat on this chair? (lay, lie)
35. She was ..... herself in the mirror. (admiring, admiring at)

B. Make up sentences of your own, each sentence including one of the following words or phrases. In the case of a verb, any tense may be used, and, in the case of a noun, a plural form may be used if a plural is possible.

(*a*) lend, (*b*) congratulate, (*c*) damage,
(*d*) furniture, (*e*) shortly, (*f*) refuse,
(*g*) deal (verb), (*h*) deny, (*i*) high,
(*j*) lie (verb), (*k*) no sooner, (*l*) obey,
(*m*) past, (*n*) remember, (*o*) scarcely,
(*p*) say, (*q*) learn, (*r*) used to.
(*s*) win, (*t*) admire,

C. Explain the difference of meaning between the two sentences in each of the following pairs.

(*a*) The bandits stole the mail van.
The bandits robbed the mail van.
(*b*) My son wishes to become a doctor.
My son hopes to become a doctor.
(*c*) I never lend money.
I never borrow money.
(*d*) I will explain the matter to you shortly.
I will explain the matter to you briefly.
(*e*) He was struck on the head by a stone.
He was struck on the head with a stone.

D. Insert the appropriate part of the verb *to buy* or *to sell* in the following sentences.

a My shoes are worn out; I must ..... another pair.
b I should have liked to ..... the house, but I could not afford to pay the price that was asked.
c A butcher ..... meat.
d I am going into this shop to ..... some cigarettes.
e We have ..... our old car, and ..... a new one.
f She had to ..... some of her jewellery in order to pay her debts.

39. The courtesy words *please* and *thank you*

1 *Please* is used after a request or after a sentence which has the force of a request; *thank you* expresses gratitude when the request is granted or complied with.

> Would you pass me the telephone directory, please?
> (*The directory is passed.*)
> Thank you.

Thank you is also the recognised formula on acceptance of something that is given without its being requested, e.g. when one receives change from a shopkeeper.

2 *Thank you* may be used in speech or in writing to express one's appreciation of a favour or kindness.

> Thank you for giving us such an enjoyable holiday.

Thank you very much is felt to be stronger than the plain *thank you*.

3 In speech, *please* is usually added at the end of a request. In writing and in public notices it is placed at the beginning if the request takes the form of an imperative.

> Please close the door.

It is incorporated in the sentence if the request takes the form of a question.

> Will patrons please refrain from smoking?

4 In replies to enquiries or invitations, *please* can be used only with an affirmative answer (Yes, please); but *thank you* may be used with either an affirmative or a negative. (Yes, thank you. No, thank you.)

5 *Yes, please* accepts an offer or suggestion and often has the force of a request:

> Will you have another cup of tea?
> Yes, please.

The opposite idea is expressed by *No, thank you*. *Yes, thank you* confirms an inquiry:

> Is your tea sweet enough?
> Yes, thank you.

EXERCISES

1 Fill in the blank spaces in the following sentences with either *please* or *thank you*.

a Will you close the window .....?
b ..... keep off the grass.
c ..... for replying to my letter so promptly.
d Could you tell me the time .....?
e How are you feeling today? Much better, ...
f ..... give my congratulations to your son on his success in his recent examination.
g Will you ..... send me particulars of your tours to Britain?
h We can do without your help, ...
i ..... for the very valuable assistance you gave me.
j Close the door behind you, ...

2 Reply to the following questions in the negative or the affirmative, as indicated, using *yes* or *no*, with either *please* or *thank you*.

a Are you quite comfortable in that chair? (affirmative reply)
b Would you like another piece of cake? (affirmative reply)
c Do you need any more money? (negative reply)
d Is your wife quite well? (affirmative reply)
e Have you enough milk in your tea? (affirmative reply)
f Shall I post this letter for you? (affirmative reply)
g I'm going to have a drink before we set off. Would you like one? (negative reply)
h Won't you have some more coffee? (negative reply)
i Is it warm enough for you in this room? (affirmative reply)
j Would you like me to telephone your aunt for you? (affirmative reply)

40. Dates and the time

1 DATES. We may write either 27 *July*, *July* 27, or *July* 27*th*. The first method is preferable. They are read as follows.

Written	*Read*
27 July	the twenty-seventh of July
July 27	July twenty-seven (or *the twenty-seventh*)
July 27th	July the twenty-seventh

For days numbered 1 to 9 the second method is less used. For years the following points should be noted.

(*a*) For dates 1000 and later the number is read as so many hundred. 1700=seventeen hundred (not *one thousand, seven hundred*).

(*b*) When the hundreds are followed by the figures 01 to 09, the usual method in reading or speaking is to insert the word *hundred*. Thus 1703 is read as *seventeen hundred and three*, not as *seventeen three*.

(*c*) When the hundreds are followed by a number denoting ten or more, the word *hundred* may also be inserted in reading, but the general tendency is to omit it. 1066=*ten sixty-six*; 1815=*eighteen fifteen*; 1914=*nineteen fourteen*.

The following table gives some examples.

Written	*Read*
1100	eleven hundred
1900	nineteen hundred
1904	nineteen hundred and four
1608	sixteen hundred and eight
1215	twelve fifteen
1662	sixteen sixty-two
1984	nineteen eighty-four

Dates are sometimes written merely as three numbers separated by oblique strokes: 3/8/63. This method is not recommended except in special cases (on forms that are specially ruled for it). One difficulty is that British practice differs from American in this matter. The former uses the order day-month-year, the latter month-day-year. Thus to a British person 3/8/63 means August 3rd, 1963; to an American it means March 8th, 1963.

2 THE TIME. There are two methods of expressing the time. They are as follows.

(*a*) By figures: 5.03, 6.30, 7.35. This is the method used in time-tables and official notices. The minutes are always given in relation to the previous hour. Thus any time between six and seven is six-something (6.23, 6.42, 6.57).

(*b*) The conversational method, in which words are used: *half past ten*, *five past two*, *ten to three*. In this method the minutes up to thirty are expressed in relation to the preceding hour, as so many *past* that hour; those from thirty onwards are related to the next hour, and expressed as so many minutes *to* that hour (i.e., short of it). Thus in ordinary speech 1.50 would be *ten minutes to two*, and 5.43 *seventeen minutes to six*.

Fifteen minutes past the hour is always called *quarter past*, and thirty minutes past is *half past*. Forty-five minutes past a particular hour is *quarter to* the next hour. For five, ten, twenty and twenty-five minutes (either past or to an hour), the actual word *minutes* may be omitted (and usually is), but for others it must be inserted. The exact hour is expressed by using the words *o'clock* (short for *of the clock*) after the number: *eleven o'clock*. But the words *o'clock* are never used when a statement of minutes precedes the hour: *five past eleven*, not *five past eleven o'clock*.

Midnight may be used in spoken English to indicate the hour: *We did not get home until midnight*; but *noon* is not generally used for this purpose. We should say *I will meet you at twelve o'clock*. not *I will meet you at noon*.

A.M. and *P.M.* In the more formal method (*a*) times between 12 midnight and 12 noon are denoted by the initials *a.m.* (abbreviations of the Latin words *ante meridiem* =before midday), and those from 12 noon to the following midnight by *p.m.* (*post meridiem*=after midday). But in ordinary spoken English these are not generally used. Instead we indicate the part of the day: *half past ten in the morning*, *half past ten at night*, *three o'clock in the afternoon*. Midnight is often spoken of as *twelve o'clock at night*.

The following table will probably be found useful.

Figures	*Read*	*Conversational Form*
11.0	eleven o'clock	eleven o'clock
11.03	eleven three	three minutes past eleven
11.05	eleven five	five (minutes) past eleven
11.15	eleven fifteen	quarter past eleven
11.25	eleven twenty-five	twenty-five (minutes) past eleven: or five and twenty past eleven.
11.30	eleven thirty	half past eleven
11.35	eleven thirty-five	twenty-five (minutes) to twelve: or five and twenty to twelve
11.40	eleven forty	twenty (minutes) to twelve
11.45	eleven forty-five	quarter to twelve
11.55	eleven fifty-five	five (minutes) to twelve
11.57	eleven fifty-seven	three minutes to twelve
12.0	twelve o'clock	twelve o'clock

EXERCISES

1 Read the following dates, or write down the words you would use if you read them aloud.

(*a*) August 27; January 1st; 17 October; May 5; 12 February; September 16th; March 3rd; November 11th; 21 April; June 23.

(*b*) 1415, 1893, 1601, 1964, 1745, 1500, 55 B.C., 1910, 1807, 1300.

(*c*) July 27, 1952; April 16, 1893; 14 February, 1946; 12 May, 1765; October 28th, 1906.

2 Give the conversational equivalents of the following times: 8.43; 12.30; 9.10; 10.15; 6.13; 7.45; 2.55; 3.40; 1.38; 10.0.

3 Express the following in the form of figures:
Three minutes past six; quarter past four; half past seven; twenty to eight; twenty-five to nine; ten o'clock; eight minutes past three; five minutes to one; seven minutes to eleven; half past five.

41. The British monetary system

1 *The system* The basis of the British monetary system is the *pound* (represented by the symbol £). For years this was sub-divided into twenty *shillings* (*s*) and the shilling in its turn divided into twelve *pence* (*d*) or *pennies*.

But on 15 February 1971 Britain changed to decimal currency. The old system of £–s–d gave way to a pound-penny (£–*p*) system. The pound was retained and divided into a hundred *pence* (*p*).

100p = £1

2 *Coins* To shop in Britain you use the following copper (in fact bronze) coins, which have been used since 15 February 1971

the halfpenny (½p)
the one penny (1p)
the two penny piece (2p)
(called two pence)

silver (in fact cupro-nickel) coins
five pence (5p)
ten pence (10p)

fifty pence (50p). This takes the place of the old ten-shilling note and is the first seven-sided coin in use anywhere in the world.

3 *Notes* Paper notes are used for higher denominations. The principal ones are the pound note, the five-pound note and the ten-pound note. Notes for even higher denominations are not in general use.

4 *Methods of writing and reading sums of money* Only one symbol should ever be written in the new currency: £6·05 (six pounds, five pence), 36p (thirty-six pence). It is important to remember that two digits must be written after the decimal point: £1·50 (one pound, fifty pence), £1·05 (one pound, five pence). The decimal point should be opposite the middle of the figures wherever possible, and not on the base line. When writing cheques, however, a dash should be used instead of a point. For cheques and in business generally it is recommended to write £0·50 (£0–50) instead of 50p. A halfpenny is usually written as a fraction: 36½p.

In the following examples the first column gives sums of money, the second tells how they would be read.

½p	one halfpenny
1p	one penny
2p	two pence
£1·05	one pound, five pence
£1·50	one pound, fifty pence

EXERCISES

1 Read the following sums of money, or write down the words you would use in reading them.

£2·32; 61½p; £27·04; £0·05.

2 A school is producing a play. The price of the tickets is 20p for adults and 10p for children. One of the pupils sells twelve adults' tickets and seven children's. How much money will he have to hand over to the treasurer?

3 Mrs Jones found one of her old grocery orders: a pound of butter for 54p, half a pound of coffee for £1·98, a loaf of bread for 29p and three boxes of matches at 3p each. How much did her bill come to?

4 I have in my wallet three pound notes and one five-pound note, and in my pocket a fifty pence piece, five 'ten pence', four 'five pence', and three 'two pence' pieces, one penny and four halfpennies. How much money have I altogether?

5 The petrol that Mr Jones uses in his car costs 80p a gallon. On a certain journey he uses $2\frac{1}{2}$ gallons. How much will the petrol for that journey have cost him?

42. Greetings and salutations

Good morning: Good afternoon These may be said either on meeting or on parting.

Good evening Usually used only on meeting. On parting during the evening, people usually say *Good night*. (See the next entry)

Good night There are several uses of this. It is said:

(*a*) When one is retiring to bed for the night.

(*b*) On parting from someone in the evening. (See above).

(*c*) On parting from colleagues or work-mates, at the end of the day's work. The time may be early evening or late afternoon.

(*d*) As a greeting, in the latter part of the evening, to someone we pass in the street but do not stop to speak to.

Goodbye Used between people on familiar terms when they are parting from each other: e.g. a man to his family or vice versa, as he leaves home to go to work; close friends or relatives after a visit, or after an outing together; one person seeing another off on a journey.

Children use *goodbye* much more than *good morning* or *good afternoon* when they are saying farewell to other children or to adults whom they know well. A schoolboy would say *Good afternoon, sir* to one of his teachers, but to a class-mate he would probably say, *Goodbye*.

Good day is not often used as an actual greeting or salutation.

Farewell The same remark applies to this word as to *Good day* (above).

Cheerio and *so long*. Slang terms for *goodbye*. Used only on the most informal occasions by very close acquaintances.

Hullo! A very familiar greeting used on meeting. It would not be used to a superior or to anyone whom the speaker did not know very well, though small children would probably use it to their elders.

It can also be used to express surprise or curiosity.

Hullo! What's going on here?

Appendix I: Infinitive and principal tenses of verbs

The following list gives the infinitive, the present tense, the past tense, and the perfect tense of the commoner strong verbs in English, and of some of the weak ones which do not follow the rule of adding *-ed* to the verbal stem for the past tense and the past participle. It is felt that this will probably be more useful to the foreign student than the usual list of Principal Parts would be. Only the first person singular of each tense has been given; where the subject *I* is printed in brackets, it means that the first person singular is not normally used, though it is given here for the sake of uniformity with the rest of the list.

The infinitive is given without *to*, though in actual fact the form with *to* is more frequently used; all the student has to do is to add the *to* when necessary.

The present participle and the gerund (which both have the same form) are made by adding *-ing* to the verb stem given as the infinitive.

The past participle is the last word of the perfect tense: e.g. for the verb *to eat* the present participle and the gerund are *eating*. The perfect tense of this same verb is *I have eaten;* hence the past participle is *eaten*.

The future tense is formed by placing *shall* for the first person singular and plural, and *will* for the other persons, in front of the infinitive without *to*.

The pluperfect (or past perfect) tense is formed in the same way as the perfect, except that the auxiliary is *had* instead of *have*.

Infinitive	*Present Tense*	*Past Tense*	*Perfect Tense*
arise	I arise	I arose	I have arisen
awake	I awake	I awoke	I have awaked or *awakened*

Infinitive	*Present Tense*	*Past Tense*	*Perfect Tense*
be (see p. 208)			
bear	I bear	I bore	I have borne
beat	I beat	I beat	I have beaten
become	I become	I became	I have become
begin	I begin	I began	I have begun
behold	I behold	I beheld	I have beheld
bend	I bend	I bent	I have bent
bet	I bet	I bet (betted)	I have bet (ted)
bid	I bid	I bade	I have bidden
bind	I bind	I bound	I have bound
bite	I bite	I bit	I have bitten
bleed	I bleed	I bled	I have bled
blow	I blow	I blew	I have blown
break	I break	I broke	I have broken
bring	I bring	I brought	I have brought
burst	I burst	I burst	I have burst
buy	I buy	I bought	I have bought
(be able)	I can	I could	I have been able
cast	I cast	I cast	I have cast
catch	I catch	I caught	I have caught
choose	I choose	I chose	I have chosen
cling	I cling	I clung	I have clung
come	I come	I came	I have come
cost	(I) cost	(I) cost	(I) have cost
creep	I creep	I crept	I have crept
cut	I cut	I cut	I have cut
dare	I dare	I dared	I have dared
deal	I deal	I dealt	I have dealt
dig	I dig	I dug	I have dug
do	I do	I did	I have done
draw	I draw	I drew	I have drawn
dream	I dream	I dreamt (dreamed)	I have dreamt (dreamed)
drink	I drink	I drank	I have drunk
drive	I drive	I drove	I have driven
dwell	I dwell	I dwelt	I have dwelt
eat	I eat	I ate	I have eaten

Infinitive	*Present Tense*	*Past Tense*	*Perfect Tense*
feed	I feed	I fed	I have fed
feel	I feel	I felt	I have felt
fight	I fight	I fought	I have fought
find	I find	I found	I have found
flee	I flee	I fled	I have fled
flow	(I) flow	(I) flowed	(I) have flowed
fly	I fly	I flew	I have flown
forbid	I forbid	I forbade	I have forbidden
forget	I forget	I forgot	I have forgotten
forgive	I forgive	I forgave	I have forgiven
forsake	I forsake	I forsook	I have forsaken
freeze	I freeze	I froze	I have frozen
get	I get	I got	I have got
give	I give	I gave	I have given
go	I go	I went	I have gone
grind	I grind	I ground	I have ground
grow	I grow	I grew	I have grown
hang	I hang	I hung	I have hung[1]
have	I have	I had	I have had
	(But see Appendix II)		
hear	I hear	I heard	I have heard
hide	I hide	I hid	I have hidden
hit	I hit	I hit	I have hit
hold	I hold	I held	I have held
hurt	I hurt	I hurt	I have hurt
keep	I keep	I kept	I have kept
kneel	I kneel	I knelt	I have knelt
know	I know	I knew	I have known
lay	I lay	I laid	I have laid
lead	I lead	I led	I have led
lean	I lean	I leant (leaned)	I have leant (leaned)
leap	I leap	I leapt	I have leapt
learn	I learn	I learned (learnt)	I have learned (learnt)
leave	I leave	I left	I have left

[1] *Hanged* and *have hanged*, when death by hanging is meant.

Infinitive	*Present Tense*	*Past Tense*	*Perfect Tense*
lend	I lend	I lent	I have lent
let	I let	I let	I have let
lie (down)	I lie	I lay	I have lain
lie (tell a lie)	I lie	I lied	I have lied
light	I light	I lit (lighted)	I have lit (lighted)
lose	I lose	I lost	I have lost
make	I make	I made	I have made
...	I may	I might	...
mean	I mean	I meant	I have meant
meet	I meet	I met	I have met
...	I must	I must	...
pay	I pay	I paid	I have paid
put	I put	I put	I have put
read	I read	I read	I have read
ride	I ride	I rode	I have ridden
ring	I ring	I rang	I have rung
rise	I rise	I rose	I have risen
run	I run	I ran	I have run
saw (wood)	I saw	I sawed	I have sawn
say	I say	I said	I have said
see	I see	I saw	I have seen
sell	I sell	I sold	I have sold
send	I send	I sent	I have sent
set	I set	I set	I have set
shake	I shake	I shook	I have shaken
...	I shall (aux.)	I should	...
shave	I shave	I shaved	I have shaved
shine	(I) shine	(I) shone	(I) have shone
shoot	I shoot	I shot	I have shot
show	I show	I showed	I have shown
shrink	I shrink	I shrank	I have shrunk
shut	I shut	I shut	I have shut
sing	I sing	I sang	I have sung
swear	I swear	I swore	I have sworn
tear	I tear	I tore	I have torn
tell	I tell	I told	I have told

Infinitive	*Present Tense*	*Past Tense*	*Perfect Tense*
think	I think	I thought	I have thought
throw	I throw	I threw	I have thrown
tread	I tread	I trod	I have trodden
wake	I wake	I woke	I have waked (wakened)
waken	I waken	I wakened	I have wakened
wear	I wear	I wore	I have worn
weep	I weep	I wept	I have wept
...	I will (aux.)	I would	...
win	I win	I won	I have won
wind	I wind	I wound	I have wound
write	I write	I wrote	I have written

Appendix II: Conjugation of *to be* and *to have*

TO BE

Infinitive: (to) be *Present Participle and Gerund*: being
Past participle: been

Present Tense	*Past Tense*	*Perfect Tense*
I am	I was	I have been
You are	You were	You have been
He is	He was	He has been
We are	We were	We have been
You are	You were	You have been
They are	They were	They have been

In spoken English the interrogative form of the negative is *aren't?* (see p. 77)

TO HAVE

Infinitive: (to) have *Present Participle and Gerund*: having
Past Participle: had

Present Tense	*Past Tense*	*Perfect Tense*
I have	I had	I have had
You have	You had	You have had
He has	He had	He has had
We have	We had	We have had
You have	You had	You have had
They have	They had	They have had

INDEX

The numbers refer to pages. The symbol *n* after a number shows that the reference is to a footnote on that page.

Words, subjects and constructions which have an entire section of the book devoted to them, and which therefore appear in the Contents at the beginning, have not been given a separate entry in the Index.